AN ENTERPRISE MAP OF TANZANIA

AN ENTERPRISE MAP OF TANZANIA

John Sutton and Donath Olomi

CONTENTS

ABOUT THE AUTHORS

John Sutton is the Sir John Hicks Professor of Economics at the London School of Economics.

Donath Olomi is Chief Executive Officer of the Institute of Management and Entrepreneurship Development, Tanzania, and formerly a senior lecturer and director of the University of Dar es Salaam Entrepreneurship Centre (UDEC).

The International Growth Centre (www.theigc.org) promotes sustainable growth in developing countries by providing demand-led policy advice based on frontier research. The IGC is directed and organized from hubs at the London School of Economics and the University of Oxford and comprises country offices across the developing world. The IGC was initiated and is funded by the Department for International Development (DFID).

John Sutton's Enterprise Map Project aims to provide a standardized descriptive account of the industrial capabilities of selected countries in sub-Saharan Africa. This is the third volume to appear, following volumes on Ethiopia (2010) and Ghana (2011).

ACKNOWLEDGEMENTS

The authors would like to thank the many organizations and individuals that supported this work, who cannot be mentioned individually.

This work was, in large part, made possible by the firms' representatives, who devoted their time to meetings with the research team. The authors thank Dr Cyril Chami (the former Minister for Industry and Trade), J. Mapunjo (Permanent Secretary, Ministry of Industry and Trade), E. Sikazwe (Director of Industry) and D. Ndunguru (the principal engineer in the Ministry of Industry and Trade) for their support.

We also thank the following government ministries and agencies for providing the necessary information and data: the Ministry of Industry and Trade, the Tanzania Revenue Authority, the Tanzania Investment Centre, the Bank of Tanzania, the Tanzania Mineral Audit Agency, the Contractors Registration Board, the National Construction Council, the Tanzania Trade Development Authority, the Tanzania Cotton Board, the Tanzania Sisal Board, the Tea Board of Tanzania, the Tanzania Coffee Board, the Tanzania Sugar Board and the Tanzania Tobacco Board.

The following business associations played a key role in linking the team to companies and providing information: CEO Roundtable, the Confederation of Tanzanian Industry, the Tanzania Horticulture Association, the Tanzania Chamber of Mines, the Sisal Association of Tanzania, the Agriculture Council of Tanzania and the Leather Association of Tanzania.

Lastly, the consulting team at the Institute of Management and Entrepreneurship Development played a key role in collecting information and writing sector and firm profiles. Particular appreciation goes to Dr Goodluck C. Urassa and Khalid Swabiri.

While we have made every effort to ensure the accuracy of the descriptions in this volume, in some instances we have had to reconcile conflicting accounts and data from alternative sources. All errors and omissions are the responsibility of the authors.

ACRONYMS AND ABBREVIATIONS

AOTTL	Alliance One Tanzania Ltd
BGCL	Badugu Ginning Company Limited
CEO	Chief Executive Officer
CRJE	China Railway Jianchang Engineering Co. Ltd
DGW	Dar es Salaam Glassworks
EAC	East African Community
EU	European Union
FDI	Foreign Direct Investment
GDP	Gross Domestic Product
HDPE	High-density polyethylene
KILICAFE	Association of Kilimanjaro Specialty Coffee Growers
KNCU	Kilimanjaro Native Cooperative Union
KSC	Kilombero Sugar Company
KSL	Kagera Sugar Limited
MDF	Medium-density fibreboard
METL	Mohamed Enterprises Tanzania Ltd
MPM	Mufindi Paper Mills
MSE	Mtibwa Sugar Estate
mt	Metric tonne
NACC	New Age Construction Company Limited
NGO	Non-governmental organization
NWFCL	New World Furniture Company Limited
PATL	Premium Active Tanzania Ltd
PET	Polyethylene terephthalate
PVC	Polyvinyl chloride
SADC	Southern Africa Development Community
SBT	Sugar Board of Tanzania
SDC	Sugar Development Corporation
SMEs	Small and medium-sized enterprises
TANICA	Tanzania Instant Coffee Company
TATEPA	Tanzania Tea Packers Limited
TCCL	Tanzania Cigarette Company Ltd
TDCU	Tanga Dairies Cooperative Union

TLTC	Tanzania Leaf Tobacco Company
TPC	Tanganyika Planting Company
TPCCL	Tanzania Portland Cement Company Ltd
TTB	Tanzania Tobacco Board
UAE	United Arab Emirates
UK	United Kingdom
UTT	Unilever Tea Tanzania Limited
US	United States

AN ENTERPRISE MAP OF TANZANIA

Chapter 1

INTRODUCTION

Tanzania has enjoyed strong and sustained economic growth over the past decade. Both the agricultural sector and the industrial sector have contributed heavily to the rise in gross domestic product (GDP) over the period. Advances in production and exports have come from many different sectors, including tobacco, processed fish, textiles (curtains), steel, flour and cut flowers. If this level and pattern of growth can be sustained for another decade, Tanzania's economic prospects look bright. It is therefore timely at this point to ask, what are Tanzania's current industrial capabilities? And where have they come from?

An Export Map

This book surveys Tanzania's industrial sector (agribusiness, manufacturing and construction). It looks at each industry in turn, examining each of the clusters of firms ('sub-markets') within the industry, and focuses attention on some or all of the leading firms in each cluster. In all, we look at 50 large firms in detail; these are chosen to be fully representative of Tanzania's industrial capabilities. The focus is on what these firms currently produce, and on how they developed their present capabilities.

To put this in perspective, it is useful to begin by looking at Tanzania's exports. Figure 1.1 presents a profile of the main export industries. Gold, which contributed virtually nothing to exports 20 years ago, is now Tanzania's main export, accounting for 36% of export revenue in 2011. No other single industry has a dominant role. Gold, cashews, and fish processing together contribute 42% of export revenue (top panel). Seven further industries contribute 25% of the remainder (bottom panel). Taken together, these 10 industries account for just over half of total exports.

A total of 22 firms account for over half of total exports in 7 of these 10 industries, all of the exports in another (gold), and one-third of exports

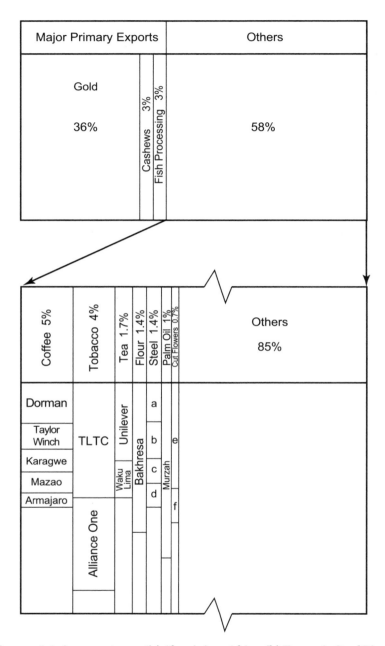

FIGURE 1.1. An export map ('a', Aluminium Africa; 'b', Tanzania Steel Pipes; 'c', Neelkanth; 'd', Nyakato Steel Mills; 'e', Kiliflora; 'f', Tanzania Flowers).

in each of the other two (cashews and fish processing).[1] These 22 firms together account for over half of Tanzania's exports.

This picture of export activity emphasizes the key role played by a small number of leading firms. Yet, in comparison with some other countries in Southern Africa, the share of total exports accounted for by the top ten exporting industries is not particularly high.[2] Tanzania's export activity is well diversified across different industries, and in two of the main export industries—cashews and textiles (curtains)[3]—a large number of medium-sized and small firms make a combined contribution to total exports that is very substantial.

The Origin of Tanzania's Current Industrial Capabilities

Where did Tanzania's industrial capabilities come from? Of the 50 large industrial companies profiled later, 29 had their origin in the domestic private sector (the remaining firms were set up by foreign firms and/or the government of Tanzania). Of the 29 domestic private-sector firms, 14 began as 'industrial startups', while 12 were set up as industrial ventures by a pre-existing firm that was already long established as a trading venture (Figure 1.2).[4]

The role of trading companies in establishing industrial operations is not particular to Tanzania: exactly the same pattern is found elsewhere in Southern Africa.[5] This pattern might seem to be attributable to the fact that trading companies have access to substantial internally generated finance. However, a study of the development of these firms suggests that two other factors may be more important. The first of these is that the trading company already has a well-functioning medium-sized organization in

---

[1] Three firms account for one-third of cashew exports. One firm accounts for one-third of processed fish exports.

[2] In Ghana, for example, eight industries account for over 90% of exports, and 27 firms account for 62% of exports. (Sutton, J., and B. Kpentey. 2012. *An Enterprise Map of Ghana.* London: International Growth Centre.).

[3] Not shown in Figure 1.1.

[4] The remaining three were set up by individuals who already operated a retail or service business.

[5] The pattern in Ghana is similar to that in Tanzania, with about half of the leading industrial firms that have their origins in the domestic private sector having been set up by traders (Sutton and Kpentey 2012). In Ethiopia, the pattern is even stronger, with almost all the leading industrial companies with domestic private-sector origins being of this kind. (Sutton, J., and N. Kellow. 2010. *An Enterprise Map of Ethiopia.* London: International Growth Centre.)

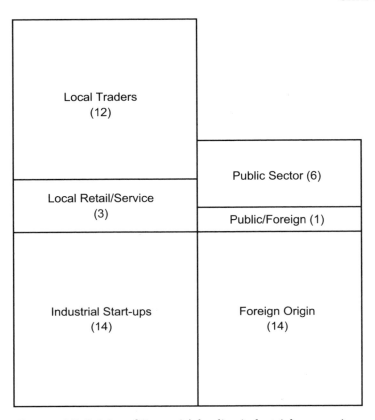

FIGURE 1.2. Origins of Tanzania's leading industrial companies.

place: the scarce resource, in other words, is 'organizational capital' rather than finance. Secondly, the trading activity builds up a huge reservoir of information about markets, and especially markets for relevant inputs, and this can give trader-led industrial ventures a substantial advantage in knowing both what can be produced profitably in the local market and how the new industrial venture can be positioned in domestic and international supply chains.

The Sources of Growth

A graph of Tanzania's real GDP over the past two decades shows a steady rise (Figure 1.3). GDP in 2010 exceeded that in 2000 by a factor of 2.0. A

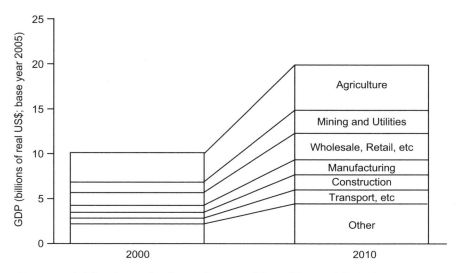

FIGURE 1.3. The change in size and composition of Tanzania's GDP, 2000–2010.

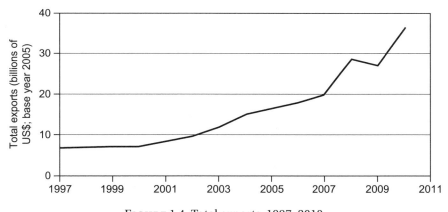

FIGURE 1.4. Total exports, 1997–2010.

breakdown of growth by sectors shows that agriculture grew by a factor of 1.5 while manufacturing grew by a factor of 2.2.

The growth of export revenue, and its composition by sector, is shown in Figures 1.4 and 1.5. Total exports grew by a factor of 5.6 in real terms between 1997 and 2010. Manufacturing exports grew by a factor of 4.0 in real terms over the same period. Gold, which contributed virtually nothing to exports in 1997, had come to contribute 32.4% of total exports by 2010.

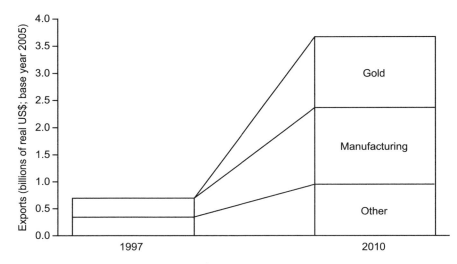

FIGURE 1.5. The changing size and composition of Tanzania's exports, 1997–2010.

Within manufacturing, the industries that made the greatest contribution to the rise in Tanzania's exports were as follows.

- Processed fish: US$53 million in 1997, US$133 million in 2010.
- Curtains: US$5 million in 1997, US$98 million in 2010.
- Non-ferrous metal waste and scrap: less than US$1 million in 1997, US$146 million in 2010.
- Steel: less than US$1 million in 1997, US$48 million in 2010.
- Flour: US$2 million in 1997, US$43 million in 2010.
- Cut flowers: US$5 million in 1997, US$36 million in 2010.

Meanwhile, one important export industry, cotton, declined in relative importance over the period.

Foreign Direct Investment (FDI)

The flow of FDI to Tanzania over the period 1995–2010 is shown in Figure 1.6. The rate of inflow rose from 1998 onwards, and achieved a ratio of FDI inflow to GDP that averaged 3.2% over the following decade (the years 2001–10 inclusive).

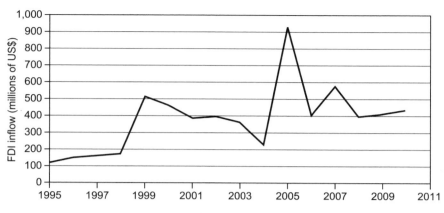

FIGURE 1.6. FDI inflow to Tanzania, 1995–2010.

TABLE 1.1. FDI flows 2005–2008, and stock (as of 2007) by sector.

Sector	Average flow (2005–2008)	Stock (2007)
Manufacturing	29.3	22.7
Wholesale and retail trade	22.3	14.6
Financing and insurance	20.2	12.6
Mining and quarrying	15.6	27.5
Utilities	8.3	6.7
Construction	2.0	4.7
Community and social services	1.3	0.6
Agriculture	0.7	2.3
Transport and communication	0.3	8.3
Total	100.0	100.0

Source: the data in this table, and in all subsequent table in this section, is taken from Tanzania Investment Report 2009 (which can be found at www.nbs.go.tz). This report was produced jointly by the Bank of Tanzania, the Tanzania Investment Centre, the National Bureau of Statistics, the Zanzibar Investment Promotion Authority and the Office of Chief Government Statistician.

The composition of FDI by sector is shown in Table 1.1. The leading sectors are mining (27% of the total FDI stock in 2007), manufacturing (23%) and wholesale and retail trade (15%).

The leading countries of origin of FDI to Tanzania are shown in Table 1.2. There are 11 countries that account for over three-quarters of the total FDI stock. (No other country accounts for more than 2% of the total stock.)

TABLE 1.2. FDI stocks and flows by country of origin.

Country	Percentage of stock	Percentage of flow (1999–2008)
South Africa	22.27	14.0
Canada	17.28	15.8
UK	13.42	22.6
Kenya	5.15	3.9
United Arab Emirates	3.57	5.3
Kuwait	3.53	5.3
US	3.49	3.9
Mauritius	3.40	15.5
Norway	2.91	4.2
Switzerland	2.70	2.4
Australia	2.17	3.5

TABLE 1.3. The sectoral distribution of FDI stock for selected countries (millions of US dollars and percentages, 2008).

Sector	Canada Value	%	South Africa Value	%	UK Value	%	US Value	%	Kenya Value	%
Mining	828.1	86.1	911.3	68.9	39.9	6.4	11.3	4.8	0	0
Manufacturing	18.8	2	82	6.2	123.9	20	98.6	41.6	78.2	45.9
Communication	1.1	0.1	1.7	0.1	9.9	1.6	4.4	1.9	8.4	4.9
Wholesale and retail trade	0.2	0	226.7	17.1	212.2	34.2	38.1	16.1	28.7	16.9
Finance and insurance	3.1	0.3	92.2	7	98.8	15.9	49.8	21	42.9	25.2
Utilities	106.7	11.1	0	0	95.9	15.5	0	0	0	0
Agriculture	3.6	0.4	0.6	0	8.6	1.4	34.9	14.7	5.6	3.3
Construction	0	0	8.5	0.6	30.7	4.9	0	0	6.3	3.7
Community and social services	0	0	0	0	0.8	0.1	0	0	0.2	0.1
Total	961.6	100	1,325.8	100	620.7	100	237.1	100	170.3	100.0

Three of these 11 countries play a dominant role: South Africa, Canada and the UK together account for over half of the total FDI stock. Inflows of FDI by country of origin over the period 1999–2008 show a broadly similar pattern to the total FDI stock (Table 1.2).

The sectoral destination of FDI stocks for five leading countries of origin is shown in Table 1.3.

Canada's investments are almost wholly concentrated in mining. South Africa is also heavily involved in mining, but has a substantial stock in wholesale and retail trade. The largest inflows into manufacturing come from the UK (US$123.9 million), the US (US$98.6 million), South Africa (US$82.0 million) and Kenya (US$78.2 million).

Challenges

In the chapters that follow, we look at the challenges facing particular industries. Many of these challenges will be familiar to readers acquainted with the economic development literature: infrastructure, power supplies, and so on.

But one issue looms particularly large in the Tanzanian context: the availability of land for industrial activity. This is an important issue, which the government of Tanzania is actively addressing through a series of recent measures. In the chapters that follow, however, the picture that emerges is more nuanced and complex than some recent discussions might suggest. In Chapter 6 for example, we encounter a small but rapidly growing Tanzanian business that has been seriously hampered by purely administrative delays (as opposed to legal or financial impediments) in transferring legal ownership of land from an individual to a company. In contrast, in Chapter 17 we encounter a new venture of substantial potential scale that captures attention at the highest levels of government. As a result, it is not only able to expand its own activities, but can provide additional fully serviced industrial plots for new local startups. So experience differs widely from case to case, and finding an effective way forward for policy on this crucial issue may require a mix of approaches and initiatives designed to tackle different aspects of the problem.

An even greater challenge in the immediate future relates to the way in which Tanzania can benefit from its oil and gas sector. Can Tanzanian firms be integrated effectively into the supply chains of the multinational oil and gas majors? Experience in other countries shows a wide range of outcomes, with some countries achieving major advances in their industrial capabilities through a successful integration of local firms into the supply chain, while other countries have almost wholly failed. Success depends on early discussions between the government and the oil and gas companies, informed by a deep shared understanding of the country's current industrial capabilities. It is to be hoped that the present volume may prove helpful in informing this dialogue.

A Caveat

The descriptive statistics presented above, in relation to the 50 leading industrial companies profiled in later chapters, must be treated with caution. These 50 firms are not Tanzania's largest 50 industrial companies; nor are they a random sample. Rather, they have been chosen as a non-random, 'stratified' sample, designed to provide the reader with a fair and complete picture of the country's industrial capability, taken across all relevant sub-markets, i.e. clusters of firms engaged in each area of activity within an industry.

Chapter 2

WIDELY DIVERSIFIED FIRMS

2.1 Five Leading Firms

2.1.1 Said Salim Bakhresa

Basic details. With a turnover exceeding US$250 million per annum, the Bakhresa group of companies is one of the largest private firms in sub-Saharan Africa, employing over 2,000 people. Its activities span three of the industries surveyed in later chapters: flour milling and bakeries (Chapter 6), bottled water and fruit juice (Chapter 7) and polypropylene woven sacks (Chapter 18).

History. In 1968, Said Salim Awadh Bakhresa opened a shoe repair shop in Dar es Salaam. He went on to open a restaurant in 1973 and by 1975 he had added a bakery and an ice cream parlour, all managed and controlled by his family. In 1983, in response to problems he faced in obtaining flour supplies for his bakery business, he set up his own wheat flour milling business. In 1988, the government decided to sell a flour mill (National Milling Corporation) as part of its privatization programme, and Bakhresa acquired the premises, replaced its outdated machinery, and raised the mill's capacity from 50 mt per day to 240.

   The firm entered the bottled water industry in 1988, expanding into fruit juices in 2006 (initially using imported concentrate but, from 2008, using fruit directly).

   The Azam PP Bags division was established in 2001 to supply polypropylene woven sacks to the firm's milling operations.

Current activities and products.

Flour milling. The flour milling operation has a capacity of 1,750 mt of wheat flour and buns, 50 mt of maize flour and 50 mt of rice per day. Average capacity utilization is 85%, with utilization varying between 50% and 100% depending on the season. Under the Azam brand it accounts for 70% of Tanzania's wheat flour production, and 80% of the turnover of the Bakhresa group. The flour business has formed the basis for the group's expansion into Malawi, Uganda, Rwanda, the Democratic Republic of the Congo, Mozambique and Burundi. It has three grain milling plants in Tanzania: namely, Mzizima Milling, Buguruni Milling and Kipawa Milling. All these are along Pugu Road and they process wheat, rice and maize. The firm also retains a line of business in baked goods (bread and biscuits). The second of the group's three core businesses is a shipping line that links Dar es Salaam to Zanzibar. The third and most recent of its core businesses is soft drinks: an operation established in 1998.

Bakhresa Food Products Ltd is based in Dar es Salaam and is part of the Bakhresa group of companies. It produces food products including ice cream, fruit juice, frozen chapattis and drinking water.

The ice cream business was the first processing activity in the group. Juice processing and water bottling came much later.

Bakhresa Food Products has three divisions: one that deals with ice cream, one with juice and the third with drinking water. The ice cream division produces Azam brand ice cream. The juice division deals with the production of fruit juices with technical assistance from Tetra Pak, Sweden. The existing plant is capable of processing tropical fruits, e.g. mango, orange, pineapple, passion fruit and guava. The Bakhresa Food Products fruit juice processing plant was Tanzania's first aseptic packing facility for fruit juices. The plant has a current capacity of 41 million litres per annum.

Bakhresa Food Products has a fully automated plant for producing non-carbonated fruit-flavoured beverages. The products it produces are packed in 300 ml polyethylene terephthalate (PET) bottles that are shrink-wrapped in packs of 12. The product is fortified with ascorbic acid (vitamin C).

The company sells its products in various countries, mostly in Kenya and Zambia. There is a plan in place to expand their market in other countries, especially Uganda, Rwanda, Burundi and Mozambique.

Polypropylene woven sacks. The Azam PP Bags division, with a plant capacity of 4,000 mt per annum, is one of the leading manufacturers of polypropylene/high-density polyethylene (HDPE) woven sacks in East Africa. It produces woven sacks in various sizes and grades, both printed and plain, for food, grain and other industrial and agriculture products.

Other activities. The transport division was established to serve the in-house needs of the group. However, it now also operates as a haulage business serving other companies. The company has over 150 vehicles, including semi-trailers, 10 tonne trucks, covered trailers, low loaders, heavy-duty recovery and tow trucks, and expandable trailers, as well as storage and warehousing facilities.

Azam Marine Company Ltd operates passenger ferries between the islands of Zanzibar and Pemba and mainland Tanzania. It has four speed-boats, built by Sea Bus of Australia, with a total carrying capacity of over 800 passengers.

SatAfrik Tanzania Limited, incorporated in May 2002, is an authorized service provider for the Thuraya Satellite Communications Company of the United Arab Emirates (UAE). (Thuraya is a mobile satellite telecommunication operator based in the UAE and operating in over 100 countries.)

The Azam Inland Container Depot is the most recently added division of the group. The services that it offers include receipt of import containers under custom bond, provision of container storage, facilitation of dispatch and the overall clearance of containerized cargo, as well as LCL ('less than a container load') shipments under its custody to designated consignees.

Organization and management. Said Salim Awadh Bakhresa is the founder and current chairman of the Bakhresa group of companies. His four sons occupy key positions. Each group company/division is professionally managed by a team of local and expatriate managers.

Firm capabilities. The milling operation uses German milling technology, which is state of the art in sub-Saharan Africa. The company is ISO 22000:2005 food safety standards compliant. The group encourages feedback from customers by allowing the sampling of test products and by making telephone and email access straightforward.

Supply and marketing chain. For its core (milling) business, Bakhresa sources maize and rice locally while it imports over 98% of its wheat requirements. The company buys maize and rice from distributors mainly from Ruvuma, Rukwa, Iringa and Uyole.

Bakhresa uses its own vehicles and network of distributors to distribute its products.

Exports. The Bakhresa group exports 20% of its output of wheat flour. The company's approach is to initially enter foreign markets through exports and later to undertake local production.

Recent developments. The factories in Dar es Salaam have undergone several major upgrades in recent years to increase efficiency and reduce waste. New initiatives include the establishment of a PET plastic recycling plant for its bottling business.

Development agenda. Bakhresa plans to strengthen its operations in East and Central Africa, and in particular it plans to build factories in the Democratic Republic of the Congo and Zambia. It is exploring investment opportunities in Kenya and elsewhere.

2.1.2 Sumaria Group

Basic details. The Sumaria Group is a regional leader in plastics, pharmaceuticals and consumer goods. It is one of Tanzania's largest private employers with a workforce exceeding 3,000, and it has a presence across Eastern and Southern Africa, as well as in India and Europe.

History. Sumaria began as a small general trading business in Kenya in the 1940s. The company was founded by K. P. Shah (who later became a member of parliament in pre-independence Kenya) and his six brothers. The firm extended its operations into Tanzania in 1957, where it started to manufacture goods it had formerly imported through Tanzania Plastic Industries. Since 1975 the company has established or acquired some 25 companies in the areas of plastics, pharmaceuticals, clearing and forwarding, food processing, edible oils, soaps, cement, wheat flour, confectionary, textiles, real estate, soft drinks, dairy and sisal. It has grown into a widely diversified multinational firm in the process.

The group's headquarters are in Tanzania and its principal shareholders are all members of the Sumaria family.

Current activities and products.

Plastics. Sumaria's companies in the Tanzanian plastics industry are the following.

Tanzania Plastic Industries. This was established in 1975 and it produces household plastic goods, furniture and rubber footwear.

Simba Plastics Tanzania. This was established in 1975, and this was followed by subsequent brownfield expansions into injection and blow moulding, and film extrusion.

DPI Simba Ltd. DPI Simba Ltd spun off its plastic piping business to form a joint venture with South African DPI Plastics (Pty) Ltd in 1999. In Tanzania, DPI Simba Ltd manufactures polyvinyl chloride (PVC) and polyethylene pipes for the civil engineering, mining, construction and agricultural sectors and is the largest manufacturer and marketer of PVC water reticulation, drainage piping systems and fittings in East and Central Africa.

Silafrica. In 2009, the Sumaria Group consolidated its diverse East African plastics holdings into Silafrica, which is East and Central Africa's premier plastics group. It encompasses three large plastic companies: Kenyan-based Sumaria Industries Ltd and Tanzania-based Simba Plastics Ltd and DPI Simba Ltd. This makes Silafrica the largest and most modern plastics group in the region. Silafrica is wholly ISO 9001 certified.

The products of the plastics businesses include the following.

Blow moulding: bottles, jerrycans, jars, floaters, buoys.

Injection moulding: round and rectangle containers, caps and closures, pipe spacers, end caps and crates.

Rotational moulding: water storage tanks, fuel storage tanks, bins, planters, material handling products, pallet bins, wheelbarrows, pallets and kiosks.

Pipe extrusion: PVC pressure pipes, PVC sewage and drainage pipes, PVC conduit pipes, HDPE polypipes (high and low pressure), gas pipes, borewell pipe casings and screens, garden hosepipes and ballpoint pens.

The group's product development centre is involved in AutoCAD product design, prototype building, mould development, mould modifications, fabrication of critical spares, and custom-designed product development services.

Pharmaceuticals. Shelys Pharmaceuticals (T) Ltd was established in 1984 in Tanzania. In 2003, it acquired Beta Healthcare International (a Kenyan pharmaceutical company formerly owned by Boots, the UK retail pharmacy chain) with the help of private equity funding from Aureos Capital, making the enlarged Shelys Africa Group the largest pharmaceutical company in East and Central Africa.

Shelys Africa is the pharmaceutical arm of Sumaria and comprises Shelys Pharmaceuticals in Tanzania and Beta Healthcare in Kenya.

Soap and toothpaste. Sabuni Detergents Ltd was acquired in 1995 from the government of Tanzania. It had been in receivership, but when the business was restarted it established new greenfield operations in soap and toothpaste.

Cotton. S & C Ginning was commissioned as a greenfield cotton ginning and cotton seed edible oil refinery in 1996 in Bulamba in the Lake Victoria region. S & C Ginning procures unprocessed cotton from farmers and gins it into bales. The company has an oil mill that produces quality edible oil from cotton seed.

Investments outside Tanzania. The Sumaria Group's interests outside Tanzania include the following companies.

Innovaxis. Innovaxis, a marketing and design company, was founded by Sumaria's African operation in 2000, relocating to India in 2006. It specializes in the design, development and manufacturing of retail vending and brand communication equipment with a strong focus on the beverage, telecommunication and tobacco sectors.

Rubicon Foods PLC. Rubicon Foods PLC, now renamed Shana PLC, was set up in 1996 in the UK, creating a new market segment in frozen ethnic foods in the country.

DPI Simba. (Described above.)

Other projects include the production of soap, cement, wheat flour and edible oil in Mozambique, and a plastics additive business using Swiss technology based in Dubai.

Organization and management. Although Sumaria is a family business, its various enterprises are managed by professional managers and technical experts. The role of family members is largely strategic, but they do play an active role on the boards of the companies.

Firm capabilities. Sumaria Group aims at world-class manufacturing and service standards. It has developed strategic partnerships with leading regional firms. A partnership with Aspen Pharmacare, the largest African pharmaceutical business, in 2008 saw Aspen take a 60% stake in Shelys Africa; Sumaria retains a 40% stake.

Sumaria was named one of the most respected companies in East Africa by PricewaterhouseCoopers in both 2002 and 2003.

Development agenda. Sumaria Group plans to expand its activities in Africa and beyond.

2.1.3 Mac Group

Basic details. The Mac Group, which is active in the the agricultural, manufacturing and financial sectors, employs over 10,000 people.

History. The history of the Mac Group can be traced back to the 1880s, when Kanji Jeraj Manek from Gujerat (India), together with some members of his family, set up a trading business headquartered in Dar es Salaam. In the 1920s, the family opened a branch of their business in the southern

Tanzanian city of Lindi, specializing in the export of cashew nuts and the import of household commodities and food products.

In 1976 two of the founder's grandsons, Yogesh and Pradip, bought a cosmetic manufacturing company called Chemi Pack Ltd. In 1978 they bought an industrial concern, Tanzania Extrusion Ltd, and began manufacturing nails and school laboratory equipment. In 1980 they set up Papcot Ltd, which produced bituminized paper, which is used to pack tobacco. In the same year Yogesh also set up PolyPax Ltd: a business manufacturing sanitary wear.

In 1981 Pradip moved with his family to Vero Beach, Florida, and expanded the family's overseas businesses. Meanwhile, in Tanzania, Yogesh established Electrodes Tanzania Ltd, a welding electrode manufacturing plant, and Industrial Chemicals Ltd, which manufactured printing inks, blackboard chalks, detergents and polishes. In 1984 he acquired Cotex Industries. (Many of the group's manufacturing businesses were later incorporated into Cotex.) In the same year he acquired National Rubber Industries Ltd: a plant in Tanga that manufactured Hawaiian slippers.

In 1985 he set up African Mosfly Industries Ltd, which manufactured mosquito coils and incense sticks; Surgicot Ltd, which manufactured surgical cotton and bandages; and Vitamin Foods Ltd, which manufactured sauces, juices and pickles.

In 1986 Yogesh and Pradip set up Mac Group Ltd as an umbrella holding company to manage the existing companies they had formed or acquired. In the same year, Mac Group acquired Tanzania Bottlers, a Coca-Cola bottling plant in Dar es Salaam. This business was extended by setting up plants in Mtwara, Mbeya and Zanzibar, and by establishing a national distribution network. Nufaika Distributors Ltd was set up to handle fast-moving consumer goods. In 1994 the Coca-Cola business was sold to the South African Bottling Company.

In 2000 the group merged two of its manufacturing companies, Chemi Pack Ltd and Cotex Industries Ltd, to create ChemiCotex Industries Ltd. The aim of this was to combine the group's industrial companies to benefit from economies of scale and share common costs. ChemiCotex Industries Ltd is now one of Tanzania's largest fast-moving consumer goods manufacturers.

In 1999 the group bought Nyanza Mines Ltd near Kigoma, a formally nationalized salt mine that was offered for privatization.

In 2004 the group acquired Interchem Pharmaceutical Ltd and began manufacturing liquid, tablet and powder medications. During the same year the group acquired Milcafe Ltd, which specializes in the blending and packaging of tea and the curing, grinding and packing of coffee.

In 2005 the group ventured into the agribusiness arena with the acquisition of the East Usambara Tea Company and began growing and processing tea (see p. 18).

Current activities and products.

ChemiCotex Industries Ltd was established in 1975. It is one of the largest consumer goods companies in Tanzania, with manufacturing bases in Dar es Salaam, Arusha and Iringa. Its operations are spread throughout East Africa. The company's distribution network consists of 1,200 business partners spread throughout Tanzania, Kenya, Uganda, the Democratic Republic of the Congo and South Africa. These are regularly serviced by eight regional offices, ten depots, a fleet of 56 delivery vehicles and over 1,300 employees. It has more than 100 products, including toothpaste, lotion, cosmetic creams, petroleum jellies, hair oils and tonics, pomades, styling gels, drinking squashes, baking powder, bicarbonate of soda, sauces, jams, pickles, mineral water, toilet soaps, laundry bars, detergents, oils, confectioneries, household plastics, industrial plastics, barbed wire, chain link fencing, expanded metal and nails.

Sagera Estates Limited has five sisal plantations near Tanga in the East Usambara Mountains. It manufactures sisal fibre and yarn. The company has an annual production of over 5,000 mt of fibre and 2,400 mt of yarn.

East Usambara Tea Company operates on 14,164 hectares, 2,000 hectares of which are planted with rain-fed tea. The company produces approximately 4,000 mt of tea per annum and employs more than 3,000 people. It has been encouraging out-growers by providing plants from its nurseries at subsidized prices. There are now over 150 hectares farmed by out-growers, with a potential yield of over 250,000 kg of tea, and this area is continuously increasing. The estates are surrounded by indigenous rain forests, which were declared a World Heritage site because of their many species of flora and fauna. This has attracted an influx of ecotourists, and the East Usambara Tea Company now plans to open an ecotourist lodge on its estates.

PIL Tanzania is a joint venture with PIL shipping agents. The company provides logistics support for cargo coming from Tanzania and nearby landlocked countries. The agency handles all vessels on behalf of PIL at the port of Dar es Salaam. The fleets of containers are maintained and managed by PIL.

Minjingu Mines Ltd was acquired by the Mac Group from the government in 2001. The mines have a proven deposit of rock phosphates of

10 million mt. The company's rock beneficiation plant converts naturally occurring phosphate in powder form to a beneficiated rock phosphate, which is used as a fertilizer. Due to its unique composition, the Minjingu rock phosphate has proved to be very beneficial to cash crops like coffee, tea, tobacco and sugarcane, particularly in the acidic soils that are found across large areas of Tanzania. Minjingu exports the beneficiated rock phosphate to South Africa, Zambia, Kenya, Uganda and Rwanda. The mine has added a granulizer plant, which converts the beneficiated rock phosphate into a ready-to-use fertilizer, and has expanded its annual production capacity to 30,000 mt of fertilizer.

Nyanza Salt Mines Ltd has facilities located in the catchment area of the River Malagarasi near Lake Tanganyika. The company converts brine to salt using two methods: thermal (for fine salt) and solar (for coarse salt). It has a production capacity of 60,000 mt per annum, 24,000 mt of which are produced using the thermal process. The plant's location affords a major cost advantage in supplying the Central African region. Over 80% of the company's production is exported to the Democratic Republic of the Congo, Burundi and Rwanda.

Other interests. The group is also active in financial services (via Heritage Insurance Company Tanzania Limited, Exim Bank (Tanzania) Limited, Alliance Insurance Limited, Strategis Insurance (Tanzania) Limited and Exim Advisory Services Limited) and in construction and real estate (via the Pacific International Lines agency).

Organization and management. The group is run from a corporate head office, and the several operating companies are independent legal entities. The styles of management within the group vary from informal to formal, based on the nature of the business. All companies use a common budgetary control system that guides their operations and their relationship with the Mac corporate head office. All the group's former manufacturing operations have now been integrated into ChemiCotex.

Recent developments. Mac Group and Heritage Insurance have recently acquired Strategis Zimbabwe, becoming the largest private health insurer in Tanzania in the process.

ChemiCotex started exporting in 2009 and now has a full subsidiary in Rwanda and partner distributors in Kenya (2009), South Africa (2010), Zambia (2011) and Angola (2011). Major investment in ChemiCotex was seen in 2011, with HBSC, Satya Capital and Catalyst Principal all becoming shareholders.

Development agenda.   Mac Group plans to expand its existing operations in Tanzania while also exploring possible new areas of businesses in other countries.

2.1.4   Motisun Holdings Limited

Basic details.   Motisun Holdings has interests in steel and assembly, engineering, plastics, paints, beverages, hotels and real estate. From modest beginnings in the 1970s, it has grown to employ around 2,000 people (including about 1,600 in manufacturing).

History.   The company was founded by Mr Subhash M. Patel, who was born in Lugoba, a rural area in the coastal region of Tanzania. His first business activity was a trading operation that involved the supply of vehicle spare parts. He later established and operated a small garage in Mikocheni B, close to what is now the group's main industrial centre. While running his garage it occurred to him that small rubber auto spares could be manufactured locally, to substitute for imported replacement parts. Later he was struck by the amount of metal waste that was accumulating in his workshop—much of it from packaging materials. He recognized that this was a symptom of a wider problem, and that large quantities of scrap steel could be found locally. This prompted him to set up a steel mill to produce steel from locally sourced scrap. The operation was expanded in the 1990s in response to new investment incentives that had been introduced. This marked the beginning of a series of ventures into new areas of activity.

Current activities and products.

MM Integrated Steel Mills Ltd was commissioned in 1995 and began with a melting induction furnace with a capacity of 3 mt per day, a seven-strand steel rolling mill with an installed capacity of 15,000 mt per annum, and an engineering workshop to meet *in situ* maintenance and production requirements. From 1997 it embarked on an expansion and diversification programme in which a tube mill plant was installed and commissioned. Its main products included hollow section, black tube and pipes. The main raw materials were hot-rolled coils, which were imported. Between 1999 and 2000, MM Integrated Steel Mills commissioned and installed a plant to make corrugated galvanized roofing sheets. In 2001/02, a modern corrugated galvanization sheet plant was installed, bringing the installed capacity to 54,000 mt per annum. In order to achieve backward integration in the production of iron sheets, MM Integrated Steel Mills invested in

TABLE 2.1. Production facilities at MM Integrated Steel Mills Ltd.

Facility	Capacity (mt per annum)	Year commissioned
Seven strand steel rolling mill	15,000	1995
Tube mill plant	20 000	1997
Continuous galvanizing plants	40	2001
Cold rolling mill plant	10	2002
Wire galvanizing plant	10 000	1999

a pickling plant and a cold-rolling mill. The plant processes 2,400 mt of hot-rolled coils per month. The main plant facilities are listed in Table 2.1.

Kiboko Precoated Sheets Limited, commissioned in 2005, has an installed capacity of 36,000 mt per annum. Its products include precoated colour steel sheets in various profiles, tiles, valleys and cutters.

PNP Industries Limited, commissioned in 2002, has a 3 mt capacity induction melting furnace, a 5 mt capacity induction melting furnace, a complete set of rolling mill plant and a pickling plant fitted in 2007 to meet national and international environmental and safety requirements.

Motisun Industries Ltd is the only producer of rubber products in East Africa. It manufactures moulds and dies for various rubber products including automobile and other machine parts and accessories.

Kiboko Paints Ltd became operational in 2007. Its products include solvent-based, special emulsion and specialty performance paints, thinners, glues, putty and varnishes.

Kiboko Cold Rolling Limited was commissioned in 2006 to increase the group's cold-rolling capacity.

MM Industries Limited is an integrated plastic processing plant established in 2006. Its products include polypropylene pipes, plastic water tanks, furniture, PVC water pipes, buckets and film in rolls.

Sayona Drinks Ltd was the first Tanzanian firm to produce carbonated soft drinks in plastic bottles. Its products include juices, water and carbonated soft drinks.

Motisun also operates the White Sands Hotel Ltd, Seacliff Court Ltd and Seacliff Resort & Spa Ltd—Zanzibar.

Organization and management. One of the group's founders, Mr Subhash Patel, chairs the board of every company in the group and is also the managing director of each company. Day-to-day operations within each company are managed by an executive director, with heads of finance, administration and operations.

Supply and marketing chain. The main raw materials used by the group are imported from India, China and Europe.

The location of all the group's companies at Mikocheni enables it to coordinate activities and to pool managerial talent, technical expertise, equipment, transport and logistics. The company has developed a strong network of distributors, most of whom handle products from several of the group's plants.

Recent developments. MM Integrated Steel Mills Ltd has entered into a joint venture agreement with the National Development Company Ltd for mining of iron ore and coal, with forward integration into sponge iron, in southern Tanzania. After full implementation of this project in about five years, Tanzania will become the third country in Africa to produce its own iron ore.

MM Integrated Steel Mills has recently entered the Zambian and Ugandan market with the intention of manufacturing quality roofing sheets.

2.1.5   Mohamed Enterprises Tanzania Ltd (METL)

Basic details. METL is active in textiles, beverages, edible oils and soap, agro-processing, grain milling, food, bicycles, energy and petroleum. The group employs more than 20,000 people.

History. The firm was founded in the 1970s by Mr Gulam Dewji, who originally owned and ran a small trading company. The firm was founded during a time in which the business climate was difficult, even in areas such as trading that were not directly affected by the nationalizations of the period. Many businessmen emigrated and this created a vacuum (in Mr Dewji's own words) in which a new, younger generation of individuals like himself could find a niche. He set up a road haulage operation, with one truck, transporting produce from one town to another, and later moved into the sale of second-hand clothing.

The firm's move from trading to industrial processing came in 1998, when it established several businesses in agribusiness and manufacturing.

Some of these were new greenfield ventures: palm oil refining, soap and candles, cashew nut processing. Others involved the acquisition of an existing enterprise that was in financial distress: a sisal processor, a sugar processor, a wheat flour miller and a bicycle maker were all acquired in this period.

Current activities and products.

Mohamed Enterprises Agriculture Division, the group's sisal business, employs 12,000 of the group's 20,000 employees. It is currently barely viable though, and the group's strategy is to maintain the business in the hope that improvement in market conditions, and/or future changes in the tariff structure on semifinished and final products, will make it profitable in the long run.

A-One Bottlers Limited specializes in beverages and packing materials. Its products include PET bottles and polypropylene containers as well as soft drinks, natural fruit juices and mineral water.

East Coast Oil and Fats Limited manufactures edible oil, soaps and fats.

Mohamed Enterprises Tanzania Ltd has interests in sisal farming and processing. It has two subsidiaries in this line of business: Tanzania Packing Materials (1998) Ltd specializes in the manufacturing of biodegradable sisal bags, while 21st Century Holdings Ltd manufactures sisal ropes and fibre yarn twines for export to industrial users in Japan, India, Spain, Italy, Belgium, Holland and France.

Mo Cashew was established in 2002 to process cashew nuts for export to the US, Pakistan, Sri Lanka, the Middle East and Eastern and Central Africa.

Agro Processing and Allied Products is involved in grain milling and processes maize, wheat and rice.

National Bicycle Company specializes in the assembly of bicycles, tricycles and motorized three-wheelers. The company is among the largest bicycle assemblers in the East and Central African region.

Other manufacturing interests include three textile companies in Tanzania: 21st Century Textiles, Afritex and Musoma Textiles. (It also owns a textile company, Novatexmoque LDA, in Mozambique.)

Mohamed Enterprises Trading Division remains the largest business within the group. The trading subsidiary deals with the import of over 20 industrial and consumer commodities.

Glenrich Transportation Ltd is a transportation business, operating 1,000 vehicles including containerized trucks, semitrailers, flat-bed semitrailers and side-bed semitrailers.

Star Oils Ltd, the newest business in the group, distributes petroleum products through a chain of 200 petrol stations.

Golden Crescent Assurances Company Limited is a provider of insurance services.

Organization and management. The board of directors is chaired by Mr Gulam Dewji. The group chief executive officer (CEO), Mr Mohamed Dewji, deals with day-to-day management. Each subsidiary has a semiautonomous management team that reports to the group CEO and the board on strategic issues.

Firm capabilities. METL is one of the oldest and most successful private companies in Tanzania. Strong relationships with financial institutions enable it to access finance easily for new projects. METL enjoys considerable cost savings by sourcing inputs across its wide range of activities.

METL has significantly reduced the amount it spends on electricity by investing in alternative sources of energy using byproducts from its manufacturing operations. It has invested heavily in developing its supply chains, giving it flexibility and reliability of delivery in all circumstances.

Supply and marketing chain. METL has made significant investments in its supply chain: the agricultural arm provides a large proportion of the inputs for its manufacturing operations in textiles, cashews, sisal and edible oil. This has made its operation sustainable during times of supply shortages.

METL's factories are situated in Dar es Salaam, Morogoro and Tanga. To cope with the demands of fast-moving consumer goods, METL has developed a distribution system that operates over 150 trucks that have fixed daily routes in Dar es Salaam and the surrounding areas. The group operates over 100 retail outlets across the country.

Development agenda. METL is now planning to enter the banking industry and is also expanding its business in oil and petroleum distribution. In manufacturing, METL is focussing on consolidating its operations through upgrading its manufacturing facilities and broadening its regional presence.

Chapter 3

COFFEE AND TEA

3.1   Sector Profile

Background and overview.   Coffee was introduced into the Kilimanjaro area by Catholic missionaries in 1898. For many years, coffee was a leading foreign exchange earner, accounting for about 25% of Tanzania's export earnings. Even now, coffee accounts for 24% of the value of traditional exports, earning over US$1 billion per annum. The country produces about 50,000 mt of coffee per annum, of which 70% is arabica and 30% robusta. Almost all of it is exported. Coffee is grown by about 450,000 families, and an estimated 2 million additional people are employed directly or indirectly by the industry. Coffee provides the main source of income for 6% of the country's population. Smallholders account for 90% of total coffee production, with the remaining 10% coming from estates. Tanzania is the 19th largest coffee producer in the world.

Production is concentrated in three areas: the north (Kilimanjaro, Arusha and Tarime), the west (Kigoma and Kagera) and the south (Mbeya Iringa and Ruvuma). Northern coffees tend to be pleasant in aroma, rich in acidity and body, and have a sweet taste with balanced flavours due to mineral nutrients from volcanic soils. Southern coffees are characteristically medium bodied and have fine acidity with a good fruity and floral aromatic taste.

Robusta is grown only in the Kagera region, with all other regions producing arabica. Arabica is produced as 'Columbian washed' and commands a premium price in the world market. Virtually all (98%) arabicas are wet processed. Tanzania uses British nomenclature for grading, which is done according to shape, size and density.

There are 15 coffee curing and hulling plants, with production capacities ranging from 1.5 to 8 mt per hour. The larger plants have older equipment and are owned by cooperative unions. Most of the smaller ones are owned by multinational coffee companies and have modern technology and few employees.

TABLE 3.1. Tea production, 2003–9.

Year	Production Estate (mt)	Small-holders (mt)	Total (mt)	Destination Local use (mt)	Export (mt)	Export (thousands of US$)
2003/04	23,151	7,109	30,260	3,225	23,688	28,598,000
2004/05	23,324	8,676	32,000	4,004	19,006	27,514,000
2005/06	21,093	7,171	28,264	3,881	23,174	27,520,000
2006/07	23,997	10,973	34,970	4,737	22,429	27,559,000
2007/08	22,518	10,180	32,698	4,253	28,318	39,424,000
2008/09	22,443	9,565	32,008	4,464	26,943	37,177,000

Note: annual production differs from annual sales because some production may be stored, or wasted.

Tea contributes about US$25 million to Tanzania's export earnings, making it the fifth largest export crop after cashews, coffee, cotton and tobacco. More than three-quarters of Tanzania's tea is exported. Tea provides employment for 50,000 families and directly or indirectly involves as many as 2 million people. Tanzania is the fourth largest tea producer in Africa after Kenya, Malawi and Uganda. It produces about 32,000 mt per annum, or about 1% of world tea production. Some 23,000 hectares are planted with tea, with estates accounting for about half of this total and smallholders for the other half. Large private tea estates account for 50% of the total while out-growers, including smallholders, account for the other 50% (see Table 3.1).

There are three main tea-growing areas: the Southern Highlands Zone (the Mufindi, Njombe and Rungwe districts), the Northeast Zone (the Lushoto, Korogwe and Muheza districts) and the Northwest Zone (the Bukoba and Muleba districts).

The industry comprises three functional areas. Green leaf production is done both by out-growers and on large estates. Primary processing is undertaken by about 20 factories, distributed across the growing areas. Finally, packing is done by five licensed factories: Afri Tea and Coffee Ltd, Chai Bora Ltd (Mafinga–Iringa), Promasidor Tanzania (PTY) Ltd (DSM), International Food Packers Ltd (Tanga) and Zanzibar Tea Packers Ltd (Zanzibar).

Only a small amount of coffee is processed into instant coffee. The main producers of instant coffee are Tanzania Instant Coffee Company (TANICA) and Afri Tea and Coffee Ltd.

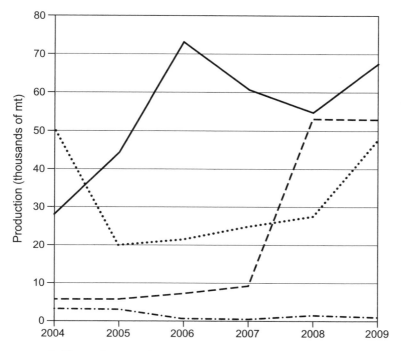

FIGURE 3.1. Coffee and tea production by type, 2004–9. Solid line: black tea. Dotted line: coffee beans (cured). Dashed line: blended tea. Dot-dashed line: instant coffee.

3.1.1 Leading Coffee Cooperative Unions

Kilimanjaro Native Cooperative Union (KNCU), the oldest cooperative in Africa, was founded in 1924 as a marketing organization for farmers in the Kilimanjaro area. It is owned by the 75,000 members of the 92 primary cooperative societies that buy coffee from farmers. KNCU is a shareholder in the Tanganyika Coffee Curing Company Limited, and in Kilimanjaro Community Bank. In 2010, its export revenue exceeded US$600,000. Tanganyika Coffee Curing Company has the country's oldest and largest curing plant, with a processing capacity of 8 mt per hour; it has over 200 employees.

Kagera Cooperative Union Ltd was established in 1950. It has 124 primary cooperatives, representing over 60,000 small farmers of the (mainly robusta) coffee grown in the Kagera region. Kagera Cooperative Union Ltd sells some of its members' coffee to the Fairtrade market, and it is also involved with the programme Export Promotion of Organic Products in Africa, whose objective is to promote innovative and environmentally sound farming techniques.

Association of Kilimanjaro Specialty Coffee Growers (KILICAFE) represents over 100 primary groups comprising over 8,000 smallholder members in Kilimanjaro, Mbinga and Mbeya. It is involved in promoting better quality, securing access to the most profitable markets, and obtaining credit facilities. It has a turnover of US$6 million, of which US$2 million came from direct exports in 2010, with the remainder being sold through the Moshi international coffee auction.

Other significant cooperatives include the Karagwe District Cooperative Union, which is also a shareholder in TANICA, and the Mbinga Cooperative Union, which owns the second largest (and oldest) coffee curing plant, with a capacity of 4–5 mt per hour.

3.1.2 Leading Multinationals

Neumann Kaffee Gruppe owns Ibero Coffee Tanzania Limited (an exporter) and two curing plants: City Coffee of Mbeya (which has 15 employees and a capacity of 4 mt per hour) and Mazao Limited of Moshi (which has 12 employees and a capacity of 1.7 mt per hour). Mazao Limited exported coffee worth about US$10 million in 2010.

Volcafe Ltd of Switzerland, the coffee division of ED&F Man, operates an export company (Tailor Winch Tanzania Limited) and a curing plant (Rafiki Coffee Ltd of Moshi, which has 16 full-time employees and 25 casual workers). Tailor Winch exported coffee worth US$12 million in 2010.

ED&F Man of Germany formerly operated both Dorman Export (Tanzania) and Gurmet Coffee Company (a curing plant with a capacity of 1.5–2.5 mt per hour). Dorman exported coffee worth US$14 million in 2010. In 2011, ED&F Man sold its interest in Dorman. (Dorman's business in Tanzania is now owned by Dorman Kenya.)

3.1.3 Local Private Firms

Burka Estates Limited is one of the largest coffee producers in Tanzania with farms covering 254 hectares. It employs 300 full-time employees and up to 2,700 casual workers at peak times. In 2010, Burka Estates exported coffee worth over US$2 million, mainly to Japan.

Tanzania Instant Coffee Company Ltd produces 500 mt of instant coffee annually. It employs more than 200 full-time staff and had sales of US$1.9 million in 2010, of which about US$1 million were exports.

3.1.4   Leading Firms in the Tea Sector

Unilever Tea Tanzania began as Brook Bond Tanzania but was later acquired by Unilever Tea. It has three large estates in Mufindi and exports most of its output, which is mostly of premium quality. Its exports in 2010 were valued at US$16 million. It is profiled in the next section.

Tanzania Tea Packers Limited (TATEPA) is one of the leading tea firms, employing over 260 full-time staff. In 2010 its sales exceeded US$19 million, of which US$12 million were exports. It is profiled in the next section.

Mufindi Tea Company, established in 1957, is a leading tea and coffee producer. Its plantations are located in the Southern Highlands, where high-quality conventional black tea is grown on the Stone Valley estates in the Mufindi area. The company produces over 5,500 mt of tea per annum and exports to the European, American, Asian and South African markets. In 2010 it exported tea worth about US$7 million. About 20% of its tea is sourced from smallholders under the company's out-grower extension scheme. The firm is Fairtrade registered and accredited by the Ethical Trading Partnership and the Ethical Trading Initiative.

East Usambara Tea Company, which is part of the Mac Group (profiled in Chapter 2), has estates that cover about 14,000 hectares, of which 2,000 hectares are planted to rain-fed tea and 450 hectares to eucalyptus trees. The company produces approximately 4,000 mt of tea per annum and employs more than 3,000 people. In 2010, the East Usambara Tea Company exported tea worth US$4 million.

Chai Bora Limited was founded in 1994 as a subsidiary of the TATEPA Group and fully incorporated in 2006 as an independent corporate entity. In 2008 it was acquired by the Trans-Century Group. Chai Bora blends, packs and markets high-quality tea. Its 2010 turnover exceeded US$10 million.

Supply and marketing chain.   The coffee sector involves three types of enterprise: coffee farms (which include estates and smallholdings), coffee processors (who operate central pulperies, currying and hulling plants), and coffee roasters and blenders. Farmers pick coffee fruit ('cherry') and deliver it to a central pulping station owned by a cooperative society or a private firm. The cherry is pulped to parchment, fermented, washed and sun dried. However, in Southern Tanzania many farmers process their coffee at home, resulting in a lower-quality (semi-washed) product. The coffee is then delivered to currying or hulling plants, owned either by private companies or by cooperatives, and is subsequently auctioned at the Moshi coffee market or sold directly to local coffee blenders or international coffee houses.

Competitiveness. The fact that most Tanzanian coffee is picked by hand and is not ground dried enhances its value on the international market. The status of Tanzania robusta and arabica coffee has improved as quality and supply have come to be more reliable, following improvements on farms, the adoption of central pulperies and increasing estate-based production.

Challenges. Productivity and quality have suffered from increasing population density (and decreasing farm sizes), crop berry disease, a collapse of extension services, ageing trees and a lack of investment in improving crop husbandry. Production costs are high relative to average world prices. Taxes are substantial and complex, involving land rent, local government levies, licenses and value added tax on fuel.

Despite stiff penalties, it is estimated that one-third of Tanzania's domestic tea demand is supplied by illegal imports smuggled into the country to avoid taxes.

Policy context. The development of the coffee sector is guided by the Tanzania Coffee Industry Development Strategy 2011–16. The government is encouraging investment in new disease-resistant varieties, new geographical areas (e.g. Karatu) and research. In order to raise quality, the government has instituted regulations that require smallholders to use central pulpery units. However, this has caused friction with some farmers, as the use of an external service cuts their net revenue by some 20% or so.

The government has issued regulations that require adoption of contract farming and establishment of stakeholder forums. However, contract farming is not seen as a viable way forward within the industry, partly because of difficulties in agreeing contracts in the face of highly volatile prices. The government is in the process of establishing a commodity exchange, which will eventually extend to coffee and tea.

The main policy bodies are the Tanzania Coffee Board, which is the industry regulator on all matters pertaining to production and marketing; the Tanzania Coffee Research Institute; the Tanzania Coffee Association, an association of coffee traders; and the Tanganyika Coffee Growers Association, an association of coffee estate owners. The Tea Board of Tanzania regulates the tea industry.

3.1.5   Leading Firms in the Coffee Sector

Two of the leading producers are profiled in the next section: TANICA and Afri Tea and Coffee Tanzania.

In 1899 a German settler founded Burka Coffee Estates at what is now Arusha's largest coffee plantation. The estate was bought by Captain J. A. Hewer, an Englishman, in 1920. He later sold it to a Swiss group of investors, who have owned it ever since, adding the Selian Estate in 1990. The estate survived the socialist era, though it suffered several setbacks, including losing some of its lands and enduring artificially high and low crop prices at various times. Since 2005, Burka has gained an export-quality certification, leading to a new export business and establishing Burka as a major brand among speciality buyers.

There are two major cooperative ventures.

Kilimanjaro Native Cooperative Union (KNCU) is the oldest cooperative society in Tanzania, with about 75,000 members from 92 local co-ops and exported coffee worth over US$600,000. It was founded in 1924 by Charles Dundas as a marketing organization for farmers. KNCU is owned by the farmers of the 90 primary cooperative societies that buy coffee from farmers in the Kilimanjaro region.

KNCU flourished in the 1950s and 1960s and drove much of the development of the Kilimanjaro region. It was nationalized between 1977 and 1984 and is still subject to government control over buying and marketing.

The liberalization of the coffee industry in the early 1990s saw private companies competing with the cooperatives to buy coffee from their members. Many cooperatives failed during this period. KNCU initially lost 80% of its market and struggled for four years. Since 1998, though, it has steadily won back market share and is now the largest buyer of Kilimanjaro smallholder coffee.

The main role of KNCU is to collect, grade, process and market coffee from its members. It also roasts small amounts of coffee for sale in the local market as well as in export markets. KNCU also owns shares in the Kilimanjaro Community Bank and in Tanganyika Coffee Curing Company Limited. KNCU also works closely with the Fairtrade movement and supplies coffee for the Fairtrade-certified 'Kilimanjaro Roasted Coffee' from Cafédirect.

In recent years, KNCU has been encouraging and supporting its members to replace ageing trees with newer, more productive and disease-resistant varieties. Nurseries have been introduced in various part of the

Kilimanjaro region to facilitate this. KNCU has also ventured into the distribution of sugar in the Kilimanjaro region.

Association of Kilimanjaro Specialty Coffee Growers (KILICAFE) is a unique type of cooperative society focused on producing speciality coffee. In 2010 KILICAFE sold coffee worth US$4 million. The association has 102 groups with 8,000 smallholder members in Tanzania's three arabica-growing areas: Kilimanjaro, Mbinga and Mbeya. It employs 17 people.

KILICAFE is a smallholder association that was launched in 2001. Its formation—and the development of its expertise in management, organization and marketing—was supported by Techno Serve, an international non-governmental organization (NGO), with funding from the US Agency for International Development.

The association's members are small-scale farmers committed to producing high-quality coffee for the specialty market. It works to support coffee growers to produce better quality, to secure credit facilities and to establish links to more lucrative markets. The association has expanded its reach over time beyond the Kilimanjaro region to Mbeya and Ruvuma.

3.2   Profiles of Major Firms

3.2.1   *Tanzania Instant Coffee Company Ltd (TANICA)*

Basic details.   TANICA produces 500 mt of instant coffee annually. It employs more than 200 full-time staff.

History.   TANICA was established by the government of Tanzania in 1963 and the factory was commissioned in 1967. From 1966 to December 1982 foreign experts appointed under a Management Agency Contract manned the factory, but since then the company has been managed by Tanzanians. In 2005 the ownership was diversified, with the majority ownership changing hands from the government to Kagera Cooperative Union, which has a 54% share. Other shareholders include Karagwe District Cooperative Union, Tanzania Federation of Cooperatives, the government of Tanzania and the firm's employees.

Current activities and products.   TANICA produces spray-dried instant coffee of different blends for domestic and export markets. These products are available both in bulk and in retail packets.

Organization and management.   The company is managed by a general manager who reports to a board of directors appointed by the shareholders. Day-to-day activities are overseen by managers responsible for production, marketing, finance and accounting, personnel and administration, supplies and logistics.

Firm capabilities.   TANICA operates the only instant coffee factory in East and Central Africa. It has won international awards on several occasions. Its organic coffee is certified by the Swedish International Foundation for Organic Agriculture Movements accredited certification body.

Supply and marketing chain.   TANICA sources beans from the coffee cooperative societies. It uses a mixture of robusta and hard arabica from the Kagera region (Bukoba). Distribution is mainly through its Dar es Salaam office. The instant coffee from TANICA is sold mostly within Africa (primarily to Kenya), but it is also available in the European, Asian and Australian markets. It is also supplied to Tanzanian supermarkets, who market the coffee under their own labels. Products are distributed from Bukoba and Dar es Salaam to wholesalers and supermarkets and directly to importers in other countries.

Recent developments.   The company has been developing new forms of packaging for small quantities, as well as looking into the production of sachets.

   A key milestone was the organic certification of its products through support from Export Promotion of Organic Products from Africa: a programme created by the Swedish International Development Cooperation Agency in 1994 to improve conditions for African smallholder farmers through developing their exports of organic products.

Development agenda.   Some foreign investors have been exploring the possibility of collaboration to scale up production.

3.2.2   *Afri Tea and Coffee Blenders (1963) Ltd*

Basic details.   Afri Tea and Coffee Blenders (1963) employs 163 people.

History.   Established in 1963 as Brooke Bond Tanganyika Ltd, the company was originally managed by the London-based Brooke Bond group of companies. Ownership was transferred to Tanzania Tea Blenders Ltd, run by the government through the Tanzania Tea Authority. In September 2002 the government sold the business to a private company, which later

changed its name to Tanzania Tea Blenders (2002) Ltd. In October 2008 the
company changed its name to Afri Tea and Coffee Blenders (1963) Ltd.

Current activities and products. The major activities of the company are
the blending and packing of teas, the packing of instant coffee powder, and
the roasting, grinding and packing of coffee beans. Its Africafe product is
a spray-dried 100% pure instant coffee powder, free of additives and made
from high-quality arabica and robusta coffee beans. The firm's tea products
include several brands and are available both loose and bagged.

Organization and management. The company is wholly owned and
managed by the Lushoto Tea Company.

Firm capabilities. Africafe appears to be the only packed instant coffee
that is exported to Japan from East Africa. The company uses state-of-
the-art machines, including a Leela Coffee Roaster from Brazil, a tea bag
machine from Maisa of Argentina, and a double-chamber tea bag machine
from IMA of Italy. It has improved its packaging by using printed inner
liners, and printed cellophane sheets, adding the date of manufacture, the
batch number and the expiry date.

   Its factory has a capacity of more than 3,000 mt per annum for tea, more
than 300 mt per annum for instant coffee powder and 750 mt per annum
for roasted and ground coffee.

   The company has an IMO certificate for the processing and marketing of
organic products. In 2002 the company received the 'Arch of Europe' quality
award in Frankfurt, Germany, and in April 2008 it became an ISO 9001:2000
certified company.

Supply and marketing chain. Afri Tea and Coffee Blenders (1963) gets
its supplies from the Lupembe tea estate in Njombe in the Iringa region,
where high-quality clonal tea is grown. It also sources tea from the Mponde
Tea Factory in Lushoto, from the Tango region and from Unilever Teas. The
company operates in 11 regions of Tanzania and supplies supermarkets,
discount stores, wholesalers, retailers and hotels.

Recent developments. Over the past ten years, the company has invested
more than US$2 million in refurbishment and new equipment.

   The company has launched several new products since 2007: Kilimanjaro Infusions herbal teas; English Breakfast Tea, Earl Grey Tea and
Iced Tea; health teas, including hibiscus, camomile, rooibos and green
tea; Africafe Safari Blend Ground Coffees (dark roast, medium grind);
Africafe Safari Blend Coffee Beans (dark roast); African Pride Tea—Gold

Blend (250 grammes); Green Label (50 gramme pouch); and Simba Chai Tangawizi (50 grammes) and Simba Chai (10 grammes).

Development agenda.   The company plans to further improve production processes and product quality, and it intends to build a second factory in 2012.

3.2.3   Unilever Tea Tanzania Limited (UTT)

Basic details.   UTT, a subsidiary of Unilever, employs 7,000 workers, mostly casual employees, at the peak tea plucking season. In 2010 its turnover was over US$16 million, with almost all revenue coming from exports. UTT's annual production of about 9,000 mt of made tea accounts for almost 40% of Tanzania's tea output.

History.   Unilever, a multinational company with a presence in many areas of the food and drinks industry, acquired Brook Bond Liebig in 1984. Brooke Bond & Company was founded by Arthur Brooke, who opened a tea shop in Manchester, England, in 1869. From there, the company gradually extended its interest to coffee trading, both in England and elsewhere in Europe, and later moved into coffee processing and growing in other parts of the world. Brook Bond merged with Liebig in 1968 to become Brooke Bond Liebig.

Brook Bond Africa entered Tanzania from Kenya in 1940 through a subsidiary called Tanganyika Tea Company, which leased tea estates in Tukuyu, Usambara and Mufindi that were formerly owned by German settlers who were interned during the Second World War.

Current activities and products.   UTT grows and processes black and green tea used in various global brands, including Lipton, PG Tips and Brooke Bond. The tea is grown and processed in three factories located in Lugoda, Kilima and Kimwele. The company also processes about 300 mt of tea per annum from nearby smallholders.

Organization and management.   The senior management team of Unilever Tea East Africa (of which the Tanzanian business is a part)—including the regional CEO and officers responsible for operations, logistics, human resources, management and marketing—are all based in Kenya. In Tanzania, there are middle managers responsible for operations who report directly to senior managers in Kenya.

Firm capabilities.   Mufindi is 1,800–2,000 metres above sea level: an ideal altitude for tea production. The tea plantations cover 3,030 hectares. Some 1,405 hectares are reserved for eucalyptus trees, which are cut on an eight-year rotation and used as firewood at the factories. About 6,000 hectares are covered with grass and other vegetation, swamps and steep land, and more than 7,000 hectares are natural forest. Most of UTT's area under tea is irrigated. Its average yield exceeds 3 mt per hectare, which is much higher than the national estate average of 2.2 mt per hectare. According to the company's management, UTT's irrigated tea area 'represents the largest known area of tea under overhead irrigation anywhere in the world'. Unilever has developed and deployed an innovative lightning detection system that allows viewing of thunderstorm activity as far as 1,000 km away. This not only increases employees safety, but also reduces unnecessary evacuations of estates and improves productive efficiency.

Exports.   More than 98% of UTT's tea production is exported. It is either exported directly or sold through the Mombasa tea auction.

Recent developments.   UTT has developed a biodiversity action plan to help preserve ecosystems in the country's Eastern Arc region. It is actively engaged in measures to improve the security of its employees, to conserve the ecological environment, and to impact local communities positively, most notably through its efforts to address issues involving sanitation.

3.2.4   Tanzania Tea Packers Limited (TATEPA)

Basic details.   TATEPA employs more than 260 full-time staff and had sales of over US$19 million in 2010.

History.   TATEPA was founded in 1995 by two long-time tea-sector workers, who acquired some of the assets of Tanzania Tea Blenders, which was then part of the Tanzania Tea Authority. The two founders partnered with the Commonwealth Development Corporation to establish Chai Bora Limited: a tea processing business. In 1999 TATEPA went public on the Dar es Salaam Stock Exchange.

The Commonwealth Development Corporation contributed to the expansion of the original business by merging it with two tea production estates: Wakulima Tea Company Limited and Kibena Tea Limited. TATEPA currently owns 75% of the stock of the Wakulima Tea Company.

TATEPA has enabled the local Rungwe Smallholder Tea Growers Association to acquire a 25% interest in the Wakulima Tea Company, to acquire

Fairtrade accreditation, and to establish an agreement with Cafédirect to supply tea for its Teadirect brand. This agreement gives Wakulima a guaranteed minimum price for made tea of US$1.45 per kilogramme. In 2006 the Commonwealth Development Corporation's 53% holding in the company was transferred to the new Actis Africa Agribusiness Fund. In 2007 TATEPA sold its Kibena tea estate, and in mid 2008 it sold the Chai Bora business to a Kenyan investment firm: Trans-Century.

Current activities and products.   Wakulima Tea Company's two subsidiaries—Wakulima Tea Company Limited and Kibena Tea Limited—grow and process tea into dried tea leaves. Wakulima Tea Company buys fresh tea leaves from smallholder farmers who are members of the Rungwe Smallholders Tea Growers Association, processes them into dried tea and sells to wholesale companies on the domestic and export markets. TATEPA sells Wakulima Tea Company's tea in the domestic market.

Organization and management.   The company is managed by an international team of professional managers. A board of directors provides oversight, under the chairmanship of the founder, Mr Joseph Mungai.

Recent developments.   Part of the business was sold recently to Trans-Century of Kenya. The main shareholder of TATEPA, the Commonwealth Development Corporation, has expressed its intention to divest the business by placing a stake of almost 50% on the market.

Chapter 4

OILSEEDS AND EDIBLE OILS

4.1 Sector Profile

Background and overview. The Tanzanian edible oil sector, including informal activities, generates over US$30 million per annum and involves over three million rural residents, primarily farmers. It is estimated that about 500,000 families in Tanzania rely on oilseed farming. The oilseeds produced comprise groundnuts (40%), sunflower (36%), sesame (15%), cotton (8%) and palm oil (1%).[1] The production volume of edible oils between 2000/01 and 2007/08 is shown in Table 4.1.

Tanzania consumes 200,000–300,000 mt of edible oil per annum, and demand is growing at 5–6% per annum. Domestic production contributes only 40% of requirements. Tanzania still imports consumable edible oil and crude oil for further processing. In 2008, Tanzanian imports were valued at US$203.6 million, compared with US$138.6 million in 2005.[2].

Major sub-sectors of oilseeds.

Sunflower. Sunflower is one of the most important oilseed crops in Tanzania, accounting for 62% of the total. It is primarily used for manufacturing sunflower oil and oilcake. The crop is adaptable over a range of environments and is widely cultivated. The major growing areas and their contribution to the total crop are Dodoma (accounting for 22.5% of total output), Singida (8.9%), Rukwa, Kilimanjaro (13.2%), and Arusha and Manyara (13.1%). Other regions that produce sunflower are Iringa, Mbeya, Ruvuma, Tanga, Morogoro, Rukwa and Coast. Sunflowers are predominantly grown by small-scale farmers on farms of 0.4–1.2 hectares. It is estimated that about 150,000–200,000 small-scale farmers are involved in sunflower growing. Large-scale farming accounts for only 10% of total production.

---

[1] Rural Livelihood Development Company. 2008. *Value Chain Analysis of Oilseeds.* Unpublished report.
[2] International Trade Centre Trade Map (2010). Available at www.trademap.org.

TABLE 4.1. Production of edible oils between 2000/01 and 2007/08 (mt).

Year	Sunflower	Cotton	Ground-nuts	Sesame	Palm oil	Soya beans	Corn oil
2000/01	80,870	124	206,800	25,707	10,440	1,430	—
2001/02	104,400	148,142	289,500	55,100	10,620	1,270	—
2002/03	112,440	187,883	255,100	22,485	10,940	2,060	—
2003/04	106,312	139,829	163,360	49,163	11,788	1,070	—
2004/05	88,854	341,789	125,311	74,989	11,098	1,150	—
2005/06	373,391	376,591	783,775	221,421	14,989	5,000	—
2006/07	369,803	130,585	408,058	155,794	15,224	3,000	—
2007/08	418,317	200,662	396,769	46,767	17,787	3,500	180,000
Total	1,654,387	1,525,605	2,628,673	651,426	102,886	18,480	180,000
Average 2006–8	387,170	235,946	529,534	141,327	16,000	3,833	—
Estimated potential production	2,650,000	4,000,000	2,000,000	1,500,000	300,000	2,166,000	1,800,000

Source: Ministry of Industry and Trade (2009).

Sesame. Most sesame is grown by small-scale farmers in Mtwara, Lindi, Dodoma, Arusha, Manyara, Iringa and Singida. Sesame is also produced in Tabora, Mbeya, Tanga and Ruvuma. Three-quarters of production comes from the south of the country. Processing is mostly carried out using small machines, suitable for serving home consumption and small-scale trading. A medium-scale sesame oil mill (with a capacity of 80 mt per day) was installed in Lindi in 2009 by Frasal Inter Trade Limited.

Palm oil seeds. Palms have been grown in Kigoma since the early 1920s. The local cooperative societies collect about 150,000 litres of palm oil annually, and they sell this to local refineries and to soap producers in Dar es Salaam. Large-scale production started in Kigoma in 2005, when FELISA Company Ltd planted its first hybrid palm seedlings. The company began operations at a 100 hectare oil palm plantation, later obtaining another 4,258 hectares on which they plan to plant oil palm. The company is aiming at a cultivation area of 10,000 hectares, half of which is expected to come from smallholder out-growers.

Palm oil seeds are also produced in Mbeya and some parts of the Tanga region. At the local level, women are in charge of boiling and milling of palm oil as well as in selling palm oil products. Additional uses for this crop have been developed more recently, including local soap production.

Soya beans. Most soya beans are produced in Ruvuma, Rukwa, Iringa, Mbeya and Morogoro. Some is produced in Lindi, Mtwara, Kagera, Manyara and Tanga.

TABLE 4.2. Sunflower and cotton seeds refining plants.

Name of plant	Location	Crushing capacity (mt)	Refining capacity (mt)
Mount Meru Millers Limited	Arusha, Singida	60,000	20,000
Murzah Oil Mills Limited	Dar es Salaam	30,000	60,000
Iringa Vegetable Oil	Iringa	45,000	10,000
Vegetable Oil Industries Ltd	Mwanza	60,000	10,000
Abood Seed Oil Industries Ltd	Morogoro	30,000	10,000
Kahama Oil Mills Ltd	Shinyanga	30,000	—
Jambo Oil Mill	Shinyanga	30,000	—
Gaki Investment Oil Mill	Shinyanga	30,000	5,000
Brown Eagle Oil Mill	Shinyanga	30,000	—
Bunda Oil Mill	Bunda	60,000	10,000
Kahama Oil Mills	Shinyanga	30,000	—
Samir Oil Mill	Shinyanga	45,000	—
Kahama Cotton Mill	Shinyanga	45,000	—
Fresho Oil Mill	Shinyanga	30,000	—
Birchu Oil Mill	Mwanza	30,000	5,000
SMEs	Bunda	30,000	—
Other SMEs		800,000	—
NSK Tanzania Ltd	Arusha	30,000	—
Quality Foods	Arusha	15,000	—
Afro Multi Pump	Arusha	15,000	—
Total		1,600,000	130,000

Source: Ministry of Industry and Trade (2009). A dash (—) denotes that figures are not available.

Cotton. Most cotton is produced in Mwanza, Shinyanga, Tabora, Kigoma, Singida and Kagera. Other producing regions are Kilimanjaro, Manyara, Mbeya and Iringa.

Groundnuts. Groundnut seeds are mainly produced in Dodoma, Shinyanga, Tabora, Singida, Mbeya, Mtwara, Ruvuma and Lindi.

Corn oil. Production of corn oil began in 2007/08 (see Table 4.1).

Edible oil refinery plants. Tanzania has 26 major manufacturing plants producing edible oil of which 22 are devoted to refining sunflower and oilseeds, while five are devoted to refining palm oil to produce cooking oil and soap. In rural areas, processing is carried out on manual oil presses. Large-scale processing is confined to Dar es Salaam, Morogoro, Arusha and Mwanza. Production levels in processing are significantly lower than installed capacity, because of insufficient supplies of edible oilseeds (see Tables 4.2 and 4.3)

TABLE 4.3. Palm oil refining plants.

Name of plant	Location	Fractionation capacity (mt)	Refining capacity (mt)
Murzah Oil Mills Limited	Dar es Salaam	90,000	90,000
BIDCO	Dar es Salaam	120,000	120,000
Mukwano	Dar es Salaam	45,000	90,000
East Coast	Dar es Salaam	225,000	180,000
Best Tigra Industries Ltd.	Dar es Salaam	30,000	30,000
Total		510,000	510,000

Source: Ministry of Industry and Trade (2009).

Supply and marketing chain.   Sunflower is bought by traders from small-scale farmers and supplied to oil mills for processing or to exporters. The oil mills then process and sell the oil locally, mainly through wholesalers. Small-scale processors either crush their own crop or buy seeds from small-scale farmers or markets. Cotton seeds are produced by ginneries. Some ginneries are part of vertically integrated plants producing cotton lint for export, cotton seed cake for sale to animal feed manufacturers, and cotton seed oil, which is distributed through wholesalers and retailers.

Challenges.   The main challenges for the edible oil sector are as follows.

- The use of recycled oilseeds that generate poor yields and are prone to diseases.
- Good agronomical practices are not followed, and this leads to poor productivity.
- Lack of strong and effective farmers' associations.
- Shortcomings in power supplies.
- The technology employed by small processors gives poor results in terms of oil extraction.
- Buyers from neighbouring countries pay in advance at fixed (often low) prices, which farmers may accept when they are short of cash.

Policy context.   The Agriculture Development Policy of Tanzania spells out the commitment of the government to

- facilitate the formation of traders' associations with the objective of setting up a marketing system;
- provide quality control services for oilseeds;
- set up an information system to link producers and traders; and
- strengthen research and extension services.

However, imports of cheap refined and semi-refined oils have made local production less profitable. One major local firm reports that it now has a bigger processing operation in Uganda than in Tanzania because of this, and because it finds the business climate in Uganda more favourable.

4.2   Profiles of Major Firms

4.2.1   Murzah Oil Mills Limited

Basic details.   Murzah Oil Mills is part of the Murzah Group. Murzah Oil Mills Limited employs 300 staff (100 of whom are full-time personnel in the oil mills plant and 200 are part time) and it had a turnover of US$117 million in 2010. (The Murzah group as a whole employs 2,000 staff.)

History.   The founders of Murzah Group, the Zakaria family, had been importers of various products to Tanzania for over 40 years. In 1997 they established an oil manufacturing plant and began producing cooking oil and soap for the local market. The company began with palm oil and then moved into soya oil production. In 1998 the company established a dewaxing plant to process a variety of domestic crude vegetable oils. The plant operation draws on technological expertise from Alfa Laval (an Indian firm), supported by technology from Tetra Laval (of Sweden). It has a capacity of 100 mt per day, which is equivalent to 30,000 mt per annum. In 2003 it established a sunflower seed extraction plant that produces about 30,000 mt of oil per annum.

The family subsequently diversified into a series of other manufacturing ventures (see below), but Murzah Oil Mills remains the core business of the group.

Exports.   Following the establishment of the East African Community (EAC) duty free zone, Murzah began exporting in 2005. A major surge in export activity occurred in 2007. The leading destination is the Democratic Republic of the Congo, followed by Burundi, Rwanda, Malawi and Mozambique. Murzah also exports some sunflower oil to Switzerland. In 2009 Murzah's share of Tanzania's exports of palm oil products stood at 93%, with exports of US$3.36 million. Murzah had 34% of Tanzania's exports of 'other oilseeds and oleaginous fruits', with exports worth US$1.12 million. Murzah accounts for 85% of Tanzania's exports of soap products, with a value of US$13 million, through two companies called Murzah Soap and Murzah Oil.

TABLE 4.4. Installed capacity of Murzah Oil Mills Limited.

Description	Capacity per day (mt)	Capacity per annum (mt)
Physical refinery for palm oil	450	135,000
Chemical refinery for soft oil	100	30,000
Fractionation plant	450	135,000
Bakers' fat/margarine	30	10,800
Toilet soap plant	24	8,600
Laundry soap plant	200	72,000
Sunflower seed extraction	100	36,000

Source: company's profile (2011).

Current activities and products. Murzah Oil Mills operates seven refineries (Table 4.4). The company produces three types of vegetable cooking oil.

The company also makes toilet and laundry soaps, vegetable cooking fat, bakers fat and margarine (produced from the byproducts of its fractionation plant).

Other companies in the Murzah Group.

Alfa Match Industries Limited was established in 2004 to produce matchboxes. Located in Dar es Salaam, the company started with an investment of US$500,000, which later grew to US$1.6 million. It began as a non-profit operation aimed at supporting widows in the neighbourhood by employing them. The company has 400 workers, most of them women, and it produces 438,000 cartons of 1,000 boxes annually. The company uses timber from Mafinga, Sao Hill, as raw material, and it imports its other inputs from Egypt, India and China. The company sells matchboxes all over Tanzania, as well as exporting some to Zimbabwe, the Democratic Republic of the Congo and Burundi.

East African Polybag Industries Limited was founded in 2007 to make packaging materials for the Murzah Group. It has 350 staff, 200 of whom are permanent. Almost 40% of the firm's output goes to Murzah Group companies, with the remainder mostly going to Kilombero Sugar, Kagera Sugar, Azania Wheat Millers and Mtibwa Sugar. Current turnover is US$8 million.

Murzah Soap and Detergents Ltd was established in 2005 to make toilet and laundry soaps. The company is located in Dar es Salaam. It has 300 workers, of whom 200 are permanent. Murzah Soap and Detergents Ltd produces 5,500 mt per annum. It imports raw materials from Saudi Arabia,

Russia, Indonesia and China. Some 30% of its output is exported, mostly to Kenya, the Democratic Republic of the Congo, Burundi, Malawi, Zambia and Zimbabwe.

SAAFA Plastics Ltd was established in 1999 to produce packaging materials for the group's oil mills. It imports its raw materials from China, Saudi Arabia, Brazil, South Korea and India. The company employs 100 workers, 70 of them permanent.

Jumbo Packaging Printing Company Limited was established in 2002 and began production in 2003. It manufactures corrugated cartons for packaging. It employs 100 workers, 45 of them permanent. In 2010 its turnover was US$7.2 million. The company obtains its raw materials from Mufindi Paper Mills and from South Africa. It sells some of its output to other domestic companies as well as exporting to Mozambique, Comoro and Burundi.

Organization and management. Murzah Oil Mills is managed by two of the group's five shareholders. The management team comprises the managing director, the director, the general manager, the factory manager, the finance controller, the marketing manager and the personnel and administration manager.

Firm capabilities. Murzah Oil Mills is the biggest sunflower oil producer in Tanzania. A high level of local demand has allowed Murzah to lower its production costs and improve its competitiveness in exporting. It has benefited from its experience in trading with other firms within the group. The company's plant and equipment come from Extraction De Smet of Belgium, a global leader in the manufacture of edible oils. The company relies on Indian experts in edible oil production for technical support. Murzah has succeeded in rasing finance from the Tanzanian Treasury via the Bank of Tanzania, as well as from the East African Development Bank and commercial banks.

Supply and marketing chain. The company imports crude polyolefin from Malaysia and limited crude soft oils from Latin America. Some 80–85% of palm oil seeds and other inputs are imported as local producers cannot supply the volume required. Imports of these inputs are duty free. To secure a steady domestic supply of palm oil, Murzah has established close links with a farmers' cooperative union in Kigoma and established a procurement centre in the region. Domestic sales occur largely via the firm's depot in Dar es Salaam.

Challenges. The main challenges facing Murzah in export markets include documentation (especially for the European Union (EU) and US markets), meeting quality standards, and high transport costs. Importing raw materials is a slow process, especially at the port of Dar es Salaam, where it takes about 15 days to offload and clear cargo from the port. This increases storage costs and causes delays in production.

Recent developments. Murzah has recently expanded the capacity of its fractionation plant from 100 mt to 300 mt per day. The new plant's equipment was sourced from Desmet Ballestra Group s.a. and from Intersonikon, Malysia. When this plant was installed, it gave the company an opportunity to process the basic raw materials of crude palm oil, which would have been difficult otherwise. The fractionation plant is also used to separate the liquid and solid fractions.

The group has invested over US$15 million in the establishment of a new business, Alfa Pet Bottlers Limited. The new firm will begin production in January 2012. It will have an initial employment level of 100–150 workers. The firm intends to have two filtration systems to purify water.

Development agenda. Murzah Group intends to expand the capacity of its Mukwano factory. It also plans to establish offices in the Democratic Republic of the Congo, Uganda, Switzerland and Zambia.

4.2.2 Mount Meru Millers Limited

Basic details. Mount Meru Millers is a leading manufacturer of edible sunflower oil based in Arusha. The company began with 30 employees and an annual turnover of US$70,000. It currently employs 400 people and has an average annual turnover of more than US$6.5 million.

History. In 1978 Mr Tarsem Chand set up in business under the name Mount Meru Petroleum Limited with a single petrol station in Arusha. Until 1993 the company concentrated on trading petroleum products and ancillary products and services. Its main business involved supplying fuel for small-scale sunflower farmers' crushing machines in Arusha and Singida. In dealing with these farmers, Mr Chand discovered that they had no reliable market for their output. He decided to set up Mount Meru Millers in order to take advantage of this opportunity. The company began with a crushing unit in Arusha but it is now totally vertically integrated: from seed extraction to refining. The Mount Meru Group has diversified its activities into several industries, and it operates across six countries

(Tanzania, Kenya, Uganda, Zambia, Malawi and the Democratic Republic of the Congo).

Current activities and products. The main product of Mount Meru Millers is edible sunflower oil. The byproducts of production—which enjoy strong demand in export markets—are seed cake and seed husk, which are used for animal feed and boiler fuel, respectively. The company also produces sunflower and corn seeds for its out-growers.

Subsidiaries of Mount Meru Group.

Mount Meru Petroleum Limited was established in 1978 to distribute petroleum and related products to retail and wholesale customers. It employs 70 people at 13 filling stations and has an annual turnover of over US$70 million. It has a total storage facility of 7 million litres spread between its several depots.

Mount Meru Logistics Limited was set up in 2000 and is one of the largest transportation companies in Northern Tanzania. As well as operating in Tanzania, it operates in Kenya, Uganda, Zambia, Malawi and the Democratic Republic of the Congo. It has a fleet of 30 vehicles, employs 70 people and has an annual turnover of US$45 million.

Mount Meru Seeds Limited was acquired from the government of Tanzania in 2003, when it was known as Tanzania Seeds Company Limited. It deals with both the foundation seed farms and certified seed production. Maize and sunflower seeds are purchased, processed, graded, hand cleaned, fumigated, packed, certified and sold. The company currently employs 30 people and has an average annual turnover of over US$2 million. It plans to establish an out-grower network of more than 100,000 farmers and promote sunflower growing over 160,000 hectares, producing 300,000 mt of sunflower grain.

Acer Petroleum (T) Limited was established in 2005 by shareholders of the Mount Meru Group of companies. It imports and distributes petroleum and related products. It employs 80 people and has an average annual turnover in excess of US$100 million. The company plans to build a new depot near Dar es Salaam Port with a capacity of 48 million litres.

Organization and management. Mount Meru Millers has a board of directors comprising all shareholders. Day-to-day affairs are managed by an executive director assisted by managers for each function. The group is decentralized, and each subsidiary is treated as an autonomous unit.

Firm capabilities. The company has an out-grower network of 70,000 sunflower farmers in the Arusha, Manyara and Singida regions. The manufacturing plant in Arusha has undergone a substantial transformation over the past six years, with the installation of automated and modern machinery that has improved productivity and quality.

Supply and marketing chain. The company's trucks collect raw materials from selling centres and deliver them to a storage facility and seed crushing unit in Singida or Njiro. The company has six sales outlets in Arusha and operates a fleet of vehicles to provide transport to several regions around the country.

Exports. The firm exports 70% of its output to neighbouring countries (Kenya, Uganda, Zambia and the Democratic Republic of the Congo) as well as exporting to Europe (particularly Turkey and Ukraine). The value of its annual exports is about US$5 million.

Recent developments. Mount Meru Millers has recently set up a seed crushing plant and a nursery in the Singida region. The firm has also set up a US$430 million plant in Uganda, which is now in operation, and it is in the process of setting up plants in Rwanda and Zambia. This expansion is being financed by medium- and long-term loans from financial institutions.

Development agenda. The company plans to double its oil crushing and refining capacity by building plants in neighbouring countries. Mount Meru Millers also intends to add another boiler that uses byproducts (husk) as fuel. The company also intends to build a silo with the capacity to store 5,000 mt of seed.

4.2.3   *Vegetable Oil Industries Ltd*

Basic details. Vegetable Oil Industries was established in 1966. The company employs 41 permanent and 250 temporary workers. The company's annual capacity is 16,000 mt. Its turnover in 2010 was US$3.4 million.

History. The founders of the company, Mr Madhubhai Patel and Mr Somabhai Patel, began their business careers as owners of three cotton ginneries: Kwimba Ginnery, Maswa Ginnery and Alliance Ginnery. They bought cotton from farmers and processed it for export. In 1967 the government nationalized the ginneries, and the former owners established Vegetable Oil Industries to buy cotton and cotton seeds from the Farmers Association through the Victoria Federation of Cooperative Unions Ltd.

Since then, the company has diversified into several different areas of business.

Current activities and products.   The group operates several businesses, including

- Vegetable Oil Industries (cooking oil, fats, plastic/cans, drinking water, battery solution and distilled water),
- Victoria Polly Bags Ltd (polypropylene woven sacks),
- Victoria Moulders Ltd (plastic injection items, plastic HDPE rolls, tyre retreading, plastic PVC pipes, liner bags and transport services),
- Hotel Tilapia Ltd in Mwanza City and
- Mbalageti Safari Camp in Serengeti National Park, Kijereshi Tented Camp in the Western corridor and Fish Eagle Resorts.

Organization and management.   The group is governed by a board of directors that includes the main shareholders. Day-to-day activities are managed by the managing director, assisted by a director for finance, an information technology manager and a country manager (responsible for marketing, sales and promotion).

Firm capabilities.   Vegetable Oil Industries was the first edible oil company in Mwanza that engaged in processing local cotton seeds and manufacturing cotton seed oil. It was also the first manufacturer of cooking fats and margarine in Tanzania.

Supply and marketing chain.   Most of the raw materials are sourced locally, with some being imported from Kenya. It delivers its products directly to its customers.

Exports.   The company exports vegetable oil to Uganda and Rwanda. It occasionally exports cotton to South Africa and Saudi Arabia.

Recent developments.   Vegetable Oil Industries enjoyed a large market share until the late 1980s but suffered some setbacks at that time due to import competition. A lack of domestic inputs, mainly due to limited rainfall in recent years, has caused the company to reduce its volume of operation and its level of employment. Vegetable Oil Industries has been diversifying its businesses, with its most recent ventures being Victoria Polly Bags Ltd and Victoria Moulders Ltd (both of which operate as independent subsidiaries).

Development agenda.   The company plans to improve its arrangements for transportation of cotton seeds from various ginneries to the plant, allowing it better control over costs and logistics. It is replacing machines: this will include two new decorticators with a capacity of 100 mt per day, and four expellers with a capacity of 50 mt per day. This is expected to increase capacity by 10% while reducing power costs by 20% and production costs by 25%. The company plans to build new godowns to provide additional storage facilities. The company plans to open a branch office in Kampala.

4.2.4   BIDCO Oil and Soap Limited

Basic details.   BIDCO Oil and Soap was established in Tanzania in 2001 as part of a group of companies that started producing and exporting oil from BIDCO Oil Refineries Ltd in Kenya. The company is part of the BIDCO family, whose operations include clothing manufacture, soap production and oil production. It employs 180 permanent workers and 300 temporary ones. It has so far injected over US$20 million in capital investment to create the most modern edible oil refinery in the country.

History.   BIDCO began in 1970 as a clothing factory in Kenya. It later added other lines of business including a soap manufacturing plant in Nairobi (1985), BIDCO Oil Refineries in Thika (1991), a seed crushing plant (1998), and BIDCO Tanzania Oil and Soap (2001). Since then, BIDCO has acquired all of Unilever's edible oil brands in Tanzania (2002), it has established a refinery project in Dar es Salaam (2003), it has launched a subsidiary in Uganda (2003) and it has continued to expand its business in East Africa.

BIDCO Tanzania was established following a market research project on the market potential for oil and soap manufacturing in Tanzania. In 1999 the owners bought a small local Tanzanian soap manufacturing firm (Shirji & Sons) and obtained contracts to supply edible oil sourced from a third party in order to test the Tanzania market. In 2003 they set up a refinery for edible oils (palm oil) using German technology. Soap production technology was sourced from Italy.

Current activities and products.   BIDCO produces edible oil, soap and fat. Soap is produced as large bars of multipurpose soap that is used for laundry, washing, dishes and bathing. The company is currently investigating the possibility of manufacturing toilet soap.

Organization and management. The company is centrally managed by a managing director based in Kenya. The Tanzania country manager is the son of the owner, and he reports to the managing director in Kenya. Other senior managerial positions, including managers for finance and marketing, are filled by professionals in Tanzania.

Firm capabilities. The company, which obtained 1400 ISO certification in 2005, has established a reputation for reliability and quality.

Supply and marketing chain. Palm sheets are imported from Malaysia and sunflowers are mainly imported from Kenya. Imports of crude palm oil are duty free. The company owns palm tree farms in Kenya and Uganda and is developing farms in Tanzania. The company also supports small-scale oil palm farmers in the Kigoma area by offering them a guaranteed market for their produce.

Exports. BIDCO exports to the Democratic Republic of the Congo and Zambia. Exports to the Democratic Republic of the Congo are handled by Congolese importers. Zambia became a viable export market when it joined the SADC in 2008. BIDCO exports directly to Zambia, where it has a depot and employs some marketing staff. Almost all the company's exports are of edible oil. BIDCO's exports in 2010 were valued at over US$7 million. BIDCO was the first firm to export edible oil products from Tanzania. Since raw materials are imported from neighbouring countries, the firm is exposed to exchange rate risk; exporting to these countries is a way of hedging against this risk.

Development agenda. BIDCO plans to strengthen its collaboration with palm tree farmers in Tanzania through the development of large-scale commercial oil palm farming.

Chapter 5

HORTICULTURE

5.1 Sector Profile

Background and overview. Horticultural crop production has always been part of agriculture in Tanzania, but the development of commercial production for export began with the export of perishable produce to Europe in the 1970s. In 1989 a cut rose industry was established and this was followed by the development of a cuttings industry based on chrysanthemums. The industry has grown from that time to occupy 208 hectares today, with annual production of 1.3 billion mt.[1]

The initial investors in Tanzanian cut flowers were Dutch nationals and companies based in Kenya, who began to invest in Northern Tanzania. More recently, there have been specialized investments in the propagation of hybrid vegetable seeds, higher-value fruits and cut flowers (other than roses).

The sector has registered tremendous growth in the past nine years, with recent annual growth rates running at 8–10% per annum, though the contribution of horticultural exports to the total exports of goods and services remains quite modest. Export earnings from horticulture increased from less than US$10 million in 2000 to US$150–160 million in 2010, with more than 300,000 Tanzanians benefiting directly from the horticultural sector. Exports mainly go to Europe. Some 75–85% of Tanzanian fresh flowers are auctioned in the Netherlands and the rest are sold to Germany, Norway and the UK. The major companies in the sector are now trying to venture into the US, Japan and the Middle East. There has also been a small expansion into the regional market of the EAC and SADC countries (see Table 5.1).

It is estimated that 500,000 hectares of land is suitable for horticulture, though the area currently cultivated is less than 5% of this total. The climate is favourable, soils are fertile, and it is possible to find locations at different altitudes and temperatures that suit the needs of different

[1] Tanzania and Agricultural Workers Union. 2011. *Factors Affecting Labor Conditions in Horticulture Industry in Tanzania.* Report.

Table 5.1. Horticultural export trend 2001–10.

Year	Thousands of US$
2001/02	63,449
2002/03	45,753
2003/04	55,624
2004/05	67,162
2005/06	111,564
2006/07	125,670
2007/08	140,340
2008/09	148,500
2009/10	159,800

Source: Tanzania Horticulture Association.

varieties of flowers, cuttings and seeds. The major horticultural areas are the Central Plateau (producing tropical fruit and flowers), the Highlands (flowers, cuttings, vegetables, fruits and seeds), the Coastal Zone (citrus and tropical fruits), and the Southern Highlands (flowers, cuttings, vegetables, fruits and seeds). Tanzania's horticultural products comprise vegetables, fruits and flowers (see Table 5.2). Roses are the dominant flowers produced for export from Tanzania, with over ten varieties being produced. They contribute more than 70% of total cut flower production.[2] Climate, soil and transport links make the Arusha and Kilimanjaro regions the main exporting areas, but Tanga, Iringa and Morogoro also have considerable potential. Several other factors have contributed to the development of horticulture in Tanzania:

(i) producers have aimed for more intensive production and higher-value crops (Kilimanjaro and Arusha regions);

(ii) changes in Tanzanian nutritional and living standards have increased local demand for horticultural food crops;

(iii) the food-processing industries have created rising demand for raw materials (juices, syrups, pulps, pickles, etc.);

(iv) the status of horticultural crops in the cash economy has increased, sometimes at the expense of existing cash crops, because in most cases they have higher value per unit area (this is true of tomatoes, passion fruit, avocados, mushrooms and flowers); and

(v) new market opportunities following trade liberalization have stimulated exports.

[2] Tanzania and Agricultural Workers Union. 2011. *Factors Affecting Labor Conditions in Horticulture Industry in Tanzania.* Report.

TABLE 5.2. Horticultural products in Tanzania.

Vegetable products	Fruit products	Flower products
• Asian vegetables	• Apples	• Roses
• Baby corn	• Avocados	• Gerbera
• Beans	• Bananas	• Aster
• Cabbages	• Blackberries	• Lisianthus
• Carrots and baby carrots	• Guavas	• Gypsophila
• Cauliflowers	• Grapefruit	• Million star
• Aubergines	• Jackfruit	• Hypercium
• Kale	• Limes	• Papyrus
• Leeks, onions and shallots	• Mangos	• Tuberose
• Okra	• Oranges	• Fern
• Peas (mange-tout, snap	• Passion fruit	• Cuttings
and snow peas)	• Pears	(chrysanthemums,
• Potatoes	• Pineapples	herbs, border plants)
• Spinach	• Raspberries	• Flower seeds
• Tomatoes	• Strawberries	

Source: TAHA (2008).

Most fruit and vegetable production is undertaken by small-scale farmers using traditional methods. The floriculture industry is dominated by eight foreign-based companies, and it creates direct and indirect employment for about 20,000 people. Five companies export vegetables, vegetable seeds and fruit.

Profiles and lines of business of large firms. The flower sector was opened up by Tanzania Flowers with the cultivation of carnations, euphorbia and amimajus in open fields for export to Europe. Five years later, two companies owned by the Bruins family (Tanzania Flowers and Kiliflora) introduced greenhouses and initiated the production of roses. By 2000 there were seven companies operating in the sector, one of which was Tanzanian owned (Kombe Roses, which is now called Tengeru Flowers). Since then, the number of companies and the area under flower production have remained unchanged.

Supply and marketing chain. The global market for horticultural products is expanding by more than 7% per annum. Regular air connections from Kilimanjaro and Dar es Salaam airports provide direct access to European and Middle Eastern markets. Preferential access to key markets under the Everything But Arms regulation, the African Growth Opportunity Act and EAC and SADC agreements has enabled Tanzania to access markets in Europe, the US and the Middle East.

Challenges. Strict regulations and standards in the importing countries place heavy demands on exporters. The evolution of multiple standards has resulted in increased compliance costs. Exports to the EU are subject to rigorous phytosanitary and environmental certification procedures.

A critical marketing challenge for small horticulture investors is getting goods to market in prime condition. Small exporters send cargo with commercial airlines; they run the risk of flight cancellation or lack of cargo space on the day. The minimum economic size for freight to the EU is about 40 mt, and most Tanzanian producers are below the size that would allow for dedicated freighting.[3] Most exporters in the Northern Zone prefer to transport their produce 250 km to Nairobi due to inefficiencies and relatively high charges at Kilimanjaro airport.

The fruit and vegetable supply chain is dominated by small farmers, who sell to wholesalers or retailers buying at the farm gate. Technoserve has been providing technical assistance and marketing support to develop the capacity of smallholder suppliers. TAHA Fresh Handling Limited provides logistical solutions and coordinates freight services to more than 300 farmers producing vegetables for the high-end domestic market.

Further problems noted by companies in the sector include the following.

- Most banks consider the horticultural sector to be a high-risk sector, and there is a general unwillingness to advance loans. This results in unfavourable loan conditions such as high collateral requirements (up to 200% of the investment), short repayment periods, short grace periods and extremely high interest rates.

- The infrastructure in most areas is poor, limiting farmers' access to markets.

- There is a shortage of trained and competent workers to engage in irrigation, spray application, quality control, extension services and small grower training.

Policy context. The Agriculture and Livestock Policy (1997) provides a framework for the development of the agricultural sector. There is no fully developed policy framework for the development of the horticulture sector. Liberalization of seed policy and harmonization of seed regulations within the EAC has facilitated improved access to quality seed by vegetable producers, from smallholders to large-scale professional growers.

---

[3] Cooksey, B., and T. Kelsall. 2011. *The Political Economy of the Investment Climate in Tanzania.* Report.

During the early 2000s, the Tanzanian Investment Centre offered a package of incentives to horticulture investors, but the implementation of the promised measures has been weak. The implementation of specific measures to encourage exports and facilitate procedures through the Tanzania Investment Centre (including the exemption of payment of duty and value added tax on inputs and investment goods, the permission to carry forward losses, the facilitation of obtaining work permits and land leases, and so on) has been far from smooth. There is still a lack of clarity over legal land rights, a problem that is compounded by the Tanzanian legal system. A number of international donors (the World Bank, the US Agency for International Development and the Dutch government) provide technical and financial assistance, including direct grants and loan facilities for new ventures, and technical assistance for developing institutional capacity in the sector.

5.2 Profiles of Major Firms

5.2.1 Hortanzia Farms Ltd

Basic details. Hortanzia Farms, a producer and exporter of cut roses, employs 450 people and has an annual turnover of over US$1 billion.

History. The company was established in 1992 by Mr Homer G. Combos as an expansion of his cut flower business in Kenya. The Kenyan business began with the growing of lisianthus and later expanded into roses. Growth has largely been financed through a loan from the Tanzania Investment Bank.

Current activities and products. The main activity of the company has been the production of fresh cut roses under hydroponic cultivation on a seven hectare site in Arusha. The company also propagates rose plants using high-performance greenhouses. Other products grown at the farm include green beans, baby corn, coffee and maize. The product mix has changed over time, reflecting market opportunities. Maize and vegetables are produced for sale on the domestic market. The changing product range is shown in Table 5.3.

Organization and management. The managing director reports to the board of the company. Departmental managers supervise the eight departments: green house, grading and packing, workshops, pump house and sprayers, propagation, security, and logistics and human resources.

TABLE 5.3. Major products offered by Hortanzia Farms Ltd.

Product	Year
Roses	1993–1995
Lisianthus	1996–2000
Coffee	Since 1993
Roses	2000 to date
Vegetables (green beans and baby corn)	Since 2006
Maize seeds	Since 2008

Firm capabilities. The business depends on the owner's established relationships with businesses in Israel and the Netherlands.

Supply and marketing chain. Over 75% of the major inputs (fertilizers and chemicals) are purchased from local companies and the rest are imported. Other imported materials include stem roses for planting. International sales are made through auctions and through direct sales to wholesalers who supply supermarkets in Europe.

Exports. Some 80% of output is made up of cut roses, which go mainly to the Netherlands, Norway and the UK. Lower-quality roses go to the domestic market.

Challenges. The administrative difficulties in procuring raw materials constitute an ongoing problem.

5.2.2 Multi-Flower Ltd

Basic details. Multi-Flower, a producer of flower seeds and cuttings and of vegetable seeds, has 500 employees. Its annual turnover is about US$3.2 million.

History. Multi-Flower was established by Mr Hans Baart with support from Mr Leeg Water and Mr Ibrahim Sewish. It began in 1995 with the production of flower seeds on a small field close to the founder's home; a small number of out-growers were also involved. Turnover in 1995 was about US$300,000, at which time the firm employed 17 people. Mr Baart had been employed at a horticultural farm, Gomba Estates (Tanzania) Ltd, and had acquired substantial experience in agribusiness. The network of contacts he had developed from his previous employment played a key role in building up Multi-Flower. The growth of the business has been financed by loans from the Tanzania Investment Bank and the government of the Netherlands.

Multi-Flower established a sister company, Vaso Agroventure, in 2004. Vaso Agroventure produces flower cuttings and hybrid flower seeds. Vaso Agroventure has 450 employees.

Current activities and products. The firm's product lines—vegetable seeds, flower seeds and flower cuttings—have remained the same since the company started, though production volumes have increased greatly.

Organization and management. The company is currently managed by a general manager, who oversees the management team. Heads of finance, human resources and logistics divide their time between Multi-Flower and two sister companies: Greenstars and Arusha Cuttings. The owner has moved back to the Netherlands, to be closer to the target market, but makes over ten trips a year to the Tanzanian business.

Firm capabilities. Multi-Flower has a close relationship with international buyers and has established a reputation for timely delivery. Multi-Flower's extension services to out-growers have contributed to its success.

Supply and marketing chain. Mother seeds and cuttings are imported from Holland. Packing materials—packets and tins—are imported from Kenya and the Netherlands, respectively.

Multi-Flower starts by negotiating prices with buyers and then decides the prices to be paid to out-growers. Contracts between Multi-Flower and individual farmers are renewed annually.

Exports. Over 90% of output by value, consisting of flower seeds and cuttings, is exported to Europe—mostly to the Netherlands. Multi-Flower produces flower seeds for 11 clients in the Netherlands, France, the UK and Germany, who themselves provide the seed stock. (Vegetable seeds are sold to the local market.)

Recent developments. There has been a recent increase in orders, as flower seed companies that formerly imported seeds from China are now ordering from Africa.

Development agenda. The company plans to begin exporting vegetable seeds to Europe. It also plans to improve production technology at the farm and to diversify its activities into new areas, including tourism.

Chapter 6

FOOD PROCESSING

6.1   Sector Profile

Background and overview.   The first post-colonial government of Tanzania invested heavily in food-processing industries, but almost all of the firms that were set up at that time had run into critical difficulties before they were privatized in the 1990s. Most of the privatized firms subsequently closed down.

Almost a quarter of all registered manufacturing enterprises are in the food-processing sector. The sector provides employment to about 58,000 people, which represents about 56% of total employment in manufacturing.[1] The food-processing industries that are formally recognized in national statistics are beverages, sugar processing, milk processing, edible oil production, fish processing, grain milling, tea and coffee, and bakeries and confectionery. This chapter covers fish processing, milk processing, meat processing, grain milling, and bakeries and confectionery. Other chapters cover sugar, beverages, edible oils, and tea and coffee.

Supply and marketing chain.   Most food processors are based in Dar es Salaam and distribute their products across the county. Products are channelled through distribution centres, wholesalers and retailers. Some processors deliver directly to retail stores, and some small enterprises deliver directly to consumers.

Policy context.   The government of Tanzania accords high priority to improving the food security and nutritional standards of its people. This has been implemented through agricultural policy, food strategy and other programmes. The policy goals are 'ensuring adequacy of food supplies, maintaining safe supply, stability and security of access to available supplies by all consumers according to their nutritional needs'. Food processing is a priority sector for the government following its adoption

---

[1] Bank of Tanzania. 2010. *Annual Report, 2009/2010.*

of the Kilimo Kwanza ('agriculture first') resolution. Despite the good intentions behind current policy, the existing legislative framework has grave weaknesses. Before the Tanzania Food and Drug Authority Act was enacted, the National Food Control Commission was responsible for handling quality and safety licences for food sellers, packagers, processors and manufacturers, importers and exporters. Food processing is currently regulated by more than 17 different bodies, leading to multiple fees, a duplication of regulatory functions, delays, bureaucracy and corruption. This has made it extremely difficult for new and smaller firms to succeed in the industry.

Challenges. The main challenges facing the sector include the following.

Poor quality of inputs. This reflects poor crop husbandry, and damage to crops due to poor post-harvest handling.

Poor access to inputs. Roads in rural areas are often hard to access. Farmers are poorly organized, and are not in a position to commit to contracts, so processors use middlemen, adding to costs. There is some price competition for inputs from Kenyans, who sometimes offer higher prices than local processors.

Lack of standards/certifications. Many processors need assistance in achieving appropriate certification to allow them to export.

Packaging materials. Packaging materials are expensive, and difficult to source locally. Only the large firms use high-quality packaging, because minimum bulk order requirements exclude small buyers.

Distribution networks. Some processors who are new to the market have found that local retail and wholesale distribution channels are difficult to penetrate, despite their products being of high quality. This is sometimes attributed to the existence of long-established networks of relationships and contacts.

Access to finance. Banks are only willing to offer short-term loans at high rates of interest.

Fish Processing

Background and overview. Tanzania has both marine and inland fisheries (Lake Victoria, Lake Tanganyika and Lake Nyasa). The country also has small natural lakes, man-made lakes, river systems and many wetlands. Tanzania controls 55% of Lake Victoria, which is the largest fresh-water lake in the world. The country produces 35 million mt of fish fillets annually. The sector contributes 1.5% of GDP[2] and provides direct employment for about 400,000 people, while supporting several million others in fisheries.

Fish accounts for about one-third of the animal protein consumed in Tanzania, with sardines being particularly important for low-income consumers. The industry generates about US$94 million in export earnings; the main export destinations are Europe, Australia, the US, Hong Kong, Singapore, Japan and the Middle East. Nile perch is the most widely processed fish for export.

More than 30 processing factories operate around Lake Victoria, producing frozen and chilled Nile perch fillets for export. More than 2,000 people are employed directly in these factories, and around 30,000 fishermen are active in the lake. The catch is iced in buyers' trucks after sale by fishermen to agents of the processing factories. One-third of the marine catch comprises sardines, small mackerel and horse mackerel. Other species include jacks and trevallies, kingfish, tuna, mullet, swordfish, silver biddies, sharks and rays, crustaceans (shrimps, lobster and crabs), octopus, sea cucumber, gastropods, bivalves and shellfish. The main markets for Tanzanian fish processed by artisanal and small-scale fisheries are in neighbouring countries and in Central, West and Southern Africa.

The major companies in this sector are African Fish Packer Co. Ltd, Bahari Foods Ltd, Blue Seas Seafood Supply, E. M. Fishing, Chain Food International Ltd, Kitamon Fishing Company Ltd, Mara Fishpackers Ltd, Musoma Fish Processor Ltd, VicFish, Mwanza Fishing Industries Ltd, Nile Perch Fisheries Ltd, Tanganyika Ornamental Fish Exporters Ltd, Tanganyika Sunshine Ltd and Tanzania Fish Processors Ltd. These companies process around 58 million mt of fish annually, exporting fish with a value of US$147,600 million.

Profiles of small and medium-sized food processors.

Power Foods Industries Ltd is an agro-processing and agriculture commodity supply company manufacturing a range of cereal flours and a recently introduced range of 'plumpynut' products. It is headquartered at Kawe in Dar es Salaam.

The company was founded by Mrs Anna Temu in 1993 as a sole proprietorship company under the name of Anna Millers. Before starting the company, Mrs Temu had graduated from Sokoine University in 1982 as a food scientist. She joined the credit department of the National Bank of Commerce in 1983 as a food-processing project advisor.

---

[2] Bank of Tanzania. 2010. *Annual Report, 2009/2010.*

In 1993 she began operations with one milling machine, but she closed down that business in 1995. She stepped down from her position at the bank in the following year and reopened and expanded her business, focussing now on soy blended flours aimed at children, lactating mothers, sick and elderly people, refugees, schoolchildren and groups affected by HIV/AIDS. These products were made by blending flour with proteins, vitamins and minerals. She developed informal distribution networks with nurses who marketed her products to patients.

In 2001 the firm was renamed Power Foods Ltd. Anna Temu travelled to South Africa, Botswana and the US, where she studied production methods that allowed her to sufficiently improve the quality of her products to obtain orders from the United Nations High Commissioner for Refugees to supply soya to refugee camps.

In 2009 Power Foods entered into a franchise agreement with the company Nutriset. This led to a large order from UNICEF, which allowed Power Foods to invest substantially in new and more advanced production equipment.

To ensure that it meets required standards, the company imports peanuts from the Netherlands, powdered milk from France and white sugar from South Africa. Cooking oil is purchased locally. The company contracts various specialized institutions and specialist consultants to undertake food testing trials, market research, and to advise on packaging and pricing.

Aiming to expand her operations, Anna Temu acquired a suitable plot of land in Dar es Salaam in 2006. However, the administrative delays in transferring title from her own name to her company took five years, and shortly before title was granted, she purchased an alternative site outside the capital, to which she will now relocate.

Jumbo Food Products Limited is a medium-sized confectionery producer, with a turnover of about US$ 500,000 per annum. It employs 50 workers.

The founders, the Zakaria family, began as importers of various products including confectionery. The confectionery plant initially made bubblegum, biscuits and hard boiled sweets. The company was acquired in 2010 by the current owners after they had been in the confectionary business for 12 years.

The company's main products are still bubblegum, hard boiled sweets and biscuits.

The company delivers products to wholesalers and retailers directly or through four agents based in Dar es Salaam. It is now expanding its sales to the Democratic Republic of the Congo, Zambia, Zimbabwe, Malawi and Mozambique.

6.2   Profiles of Major Firms

6.2.1   Vicfish

Basic details.   Vicfish is the largest exporter of Nile perch in Tanzania. The company was established in 1992. It had 50 employees and an annual turnover of $US50,000 in its first year of operation. Vicfish currently has a daily capacity of 100 mt of fish, employs 598 workers, and has an annual turnover in excess of US$30 million.

The company is part of the Bahari Bounty Group, which includes the food-processing company Bahari Foods Ltd and the agricultural products processing firm Agrotanga Ltd.

History.   The company was founded by Harkishan Bhaghat, who began his career in publishing. A business acquaintance asked him whether he could supply him with prawns from Tanzania, and this encouraged him to start his own business exporting marine fisheries products. He eventually built a fish processing plant (with a capacity of 5 mt per day) using his own capital. A major jump in the scale of his business occurred when he began selling to European fish processing plants in 1996/97: this allowed the company to export chilled fish as opposed to frozen fish. This switch improved his cash flow: the turnover time for frozen fish is 90 days whereas the turnover time for chilled fish is less than a week. The chilled product is sold and packed in a way that allows it to go directly to the supermarket shelf, as well as to restaurants for immediate use.

Current activities and products.   The main products of Vicfish are chilled and frozen Nile perch fillets. Vicfish has several sister companies: Vickfish Bukoba, established in 2005, which also exports fish; Bahari Foods Ltd, based in Dar es Salaam, which buys and sells different types of fish products from the Indian Ocean and serves both local and international markets; Hunasa Ltd, established in 2009, which buys, sells and processes maize flour; and Kukupoa Ltd, established in 2010 in Mwanza, which is a chicken processor.

Organization and management.   Vicfish is headed by the owner, assisted by a director who acts as CEO. Four major departments are headed by professional managers: production, technical, quality assurance, and engineering and administration.

Firm capabilities.   Vicfish was the first fish processing firm in Tanzania to gain Fairtrade certification (from Germany). It has Eco-label Certification from the British Retail Consortium and is an ISO 22000 company. The company has established a strong network with suppliers of fish in Tanzania's Lake Zone.

Supply and marketing chain.   Vicfish sources its fish from contracted fish suppliers around Lake Victoria.

Exports.   The company exports all its output to Europe, the US, Japan and the Gulf States. Fish imports are duty free to Europe; this is critical, since without this the business would not be viable.

Challenges.   There is currently overfishing in Lake Victoria, most of which is illegal, with the fish being shipped to the Democratic Republic of the Congo. The fishing association has created its own police force to curb overfishing. Cooperation between the governments of Tanzania, Uganda and Kenya allows violators to be prosecuted.

  The company faces substantial problems in relation to air transport. The runway of the airport in Mwanza is only 200 m long, making it unsuitable for large planes. Vicfish is often forced to send produce by truck to Entebbe or Nairobi and to then fly produce out from there. This adds significantly to its costs.

Development agenda.   The founder hopes to replicate his success in fish with a new business in organic meat, creating a complete infrastructure for exporting organic beef and chicken (both chilled, not frozen) to Europe. This will require substantial developments in the capabilities of the upstream industries.

6.2.2   Tanga Fresh Limited

Basic details.   Tanga Fresh, Tanzania's leading dairy foods company, employs 240 workers and contracts 4,500 dairy farmers to supply milk to its plant. Its annual turnover is US$4 million.

History.   Through a Dutch–Tanzanian bilateral programme in smallholder dairy extension services that began in 1985, farmers were taught and encouraged to keep dairy cattle. This led to the formation of the Tanga Dairies Cooperative Union (TDCU). In 1996 a group of Dutch farmers entered into a joint venture with the TDCU to establish Tanga Fresh, so that branded milk could be sold in the Tanzanian market. Tanga Fresh began in 1997 with a modest processing factory with a capacity of 15,000 litres a day. Following a major expansion and substantial investment, production commenced on the company's present site in 2009.

Current activities and products. Tanga Fresh produces fresh milk, fermented milk, plain and flavoured yoghurt, mozzarella cheese, butter and ghee. The 13 primary societies that together form the TDCU have over 5,000 participating dairy farmers. The TDCU organizes the farmers' purchase of heifers through a microfinance organization, Farm Friends Tanzania, which was formed by Farm Friends Netherlands, a Dutch NGO. The heifers are bred by a Dutch–Tanzanian company called Holland Dairies Ltd.

Organization and management. The management team is comprised of experienced local and expatriate staff. The general manager reports to a board of directors. There are departmental managers responsible for finance, operations, adminstration and marketing.

Firm capabilities. Tanga Fresh adheres to strict international hygiene standards and uses state-of-the-art European equipment and methods. The milk is delivered to the factory in insulated tanks and all batches are then tested before being certified for production. Farmers must be registered and they receive extensive support services; milk is tested four times before reaching the consumer.

Supply and marketing chain. Dairy farmers in the Tanga region organize themselves into primary societies that run milk collecting centres. Milk received from farmers is chilled, ready for transportation to the factory, where it is pasteurized and packed. The milk collection centre also acts as a one stop shop for farmers by providing animal feed, medicine and advice all on the same premises. All output can be sold in Dar es Salaam, where demand exceeds the output of Tanga Fresh by 50% or so.

Recent developments. To make their latest expansion investment viable, Tanga Fresh have asked the African Enterprise Challenge Fund for funds to put in place a programme to increase the production of milk from existing and new smallholder dairy farmers in the firm's catchment area. In 2010 the TDCU, together with Dutch and local partners, set up a breeding unit and a dairy farm in the Tanga region to increase the supply of heifers to TDCU farmers and to expand the supply of milk to the Tanga Fresh factory. In 2010 Tanga Fresh introduced a text messaging service for farmers and milk collection centres. Around 2,000 of Tanga Fresh's 4,500 farmers now use this service to access information about the market, new developments in the industry, animal husbandry practices and to catch up on local news. It also puts farmers in touch with vets and other support services.

Development agenda.   Tanga Fresh increased its processing capacity from 15,000 litres per day in 2008 to 31,000 litres per day in 2010 through a substantial expansion of its facilities. It intends to expand its capacity to 50,000 litres per day by 2015. In collaboration with the African Enterprise Challenge Fund, Tanga Fresh is constructing new milk collection centres as part of a cold supply chain for collection, processing and marketing. Tanga Fresh is also investing in the services of Virtual City, another African Enterprise Challenge Fund grantee, to automate the recording of milk collection and payments to farmers. This involves linking the digital scales at the milk collection centres with the accounts records at Tanga Fresh. This will increase transparency of recording and payment and will ensure the farmer is paid the correct amount.

6.2.3   Azania Wheat Flour

Basic details.   Azania Wheat Flour has a capacity of 180,000 mt per annum and accounts for about a quarter of domestic wheat flour sales. It employs 100 permanent staff.

History.   Azania Wheat Flour was established in 1998 as a trucking company by Mr Fuad Edh Awadh. Initially, the owner of the company operated five trucks, transporting goods from Dar es Salaam to upcountry regions. In the course of this business he was contracted by the Said Salim Bakhresa company to transport flour from Dar es Salaam to Arusha. Seeing the business opportunity in wheat flour, he purchased a site at Ubungo in the vicinity of Riverside in 2002 for about US$140,000, using capital earned from his transport business, and built a wheat milling plant there. The firm began with a production capacity of 120 mt per day but could not fill this capacity. Azania Wheat Flour was producing high-quality flour, at slightly higher prices than its competitors. In mid 2002 the firm changed its strategy and started using lower-quality wheat from Vietnam and other Asian countries to allow it to lower its price. This strategy backfired, as customers noticed the drop in quality and shunned the flour.

   Having realized that the main causes of the company's poor performance were inappropriate positioning of its product and inadequate marketing channels, the owner employed new staff with experience in wheat milling. In 2004 Azania Wheat Flour began using higher-quality wheat and packaging materials, particularly from Europe, the US and Canada, under the guidance of the company's quality controllers and production experts. Under the new strategy, the company's results improved, in both the local and export markets. In 2006 it established a new plant at Pugu Road with a capacity of 380 mt per day. Since that time it has continued to expand its production capacity.

Current activities and products. The company produces a variety of wheat flours: biscuit flour, home baking flour, special bakers flour, brown bread flour, cake flour, semolina flour, pure patent flour, atta flour (which is used in making chapattis and snacks), wholemeal flour and semolina flour (sooji). Byproducts include pollard bran and chick wheat.

Organization and management. Mr Fuad Edh Awadh, the owner and managing director, is assisted by a business operations manager and a marketing manager.

Firm capabilities. Azania Wheat Flour has invested in modern high-quality plant. Its newer (Pugu Road) plant uses new high-speed-roller flour mills and refining systems, which produce high-quality products.

Supply and marketing chain. About 20% of the wheat used is purchased locally, particularly from Uyole (Mbeya) and from middlemen in various regions. The company signs contracts with local suppliers so as to ensure reliable supply. The remaining 80% of wheat is imported from Canada, the US, Australia, Germany and Argentina.

Azania Wheat Flour sells its products in all regions of Tanzania as well as in some neighbouring countries. The company uses independent distributors who are also used by its competitors. Azania Wheat Flour transports the consignment from the factory to the distributors. It also serves multinational clients such as Mövenpick Hotel, Mery Brown, Temeke Confectionery and Super Loaf.

Exports. Some 30% of output is exported. The major export markets are the Democratic Republic of the Congo, Burundi, Rwanda, Kenya, Uganda, Sudan, Ethiopia, Comorro, the UAE and Vietnam.

Challenges. There are several issues affecting the import of wheat, including power interruptions and unreliable suppliers. Most shippers are reluctant to use the Indian Ocean because of piracy. Azania Wheat Flour has been incurring payments to the army of up to TZS100 million per import consignment to patrol the dock. Docking delays at the port of Dar es Salaam increase costs: the company pays the shipper a penalty of up to US$120,000 per day for delays at the port.

Recent developments. Following the expansion of its capacity, the company has embarked on a new marketing campaign, with television advertising, vehicle branding, a website that allows it to receive orders on line, and new brochures and booklets.

Development agenda. Azania Wheat Flour is planning to expand its production capacity at the Pugu Road plant to 880 mt per day. It plans to establish plants in Uganda, Rwanda and Ethiopia. It is investing in improving logistics and is integrating new distributors and agents into its network.

6.2.4 Coast Millers Ltd

Basic details. Coast Millers is one of the major grain processors in Dar es Salaam. It employs 85 permanent employees and 15 casual workers.

History. Coast Millers was established in 1992 by Mr Gupta Aggrayal as a manufacturer of wheat flour. The owner had been a long-term entrepreneur and holds shares in several companies. He has also invested in logistics and transportation businesses and in the supply of spare parts. He is currently the chairman of the Millers Association of Tanzania.

Current activities and products. Coast Millers produces wheat flour for home and bakery use.

Organization and management. The company is family owned. The owner is assisted by his son, by two chief millers, and by managers for marketing, factory operations, finance and administration.

Firm capabilities. The company uses Italian technology, which is among the best in the industry. It has a maintenance contract with the manufacturer to service its machines annually. The company has developed a good relationship with banks to support its investments in capacity.

Supply and marketing chain. The company imports 98% of its wheat from Ukraine, Croatia, Argentina, German, Russia, Pakistan and India, with local wheat producers supplying the other 2%. The firm supplies biscuit and bread factories, hotels and restaurants, as well as selling into the retail market. The company uses both direct distribution and indirect sales through agents in Same, Mwanza, Arusha, Zanzibar and Pemba. Its major local markets are in Ruvuma (Songea and Mbinga), Morogoro (Mazimbu), Dodoma, Arusha, Mwanza and Pemba. The company has a fleet of seven trucks: two operating in Dar es Salaam and five on upcountry routes.

Exports.   Coast Millers exports a small volume of wheat flour to the Democratic Republic of the Congo, Rwanda and Burundi.

Recent developments.   The company has invested about US$5 million in a new cereal store at Mbagala with a storage capacity of 16,000 mt. It has set up new computerized machines in place of older technology. It is now strengthening its sales and marketing activities. In parallel with this, it is renovating old plant and expanding production capacity. It is also exploring new regional markets within the country, and is expanding its fleet. It is also exploring export opportunities in East and Central Africa.

Chapter 7

BEVERAGES

7.1 Sector Profile

Background and overview. The beverage sector comprises alcoholic and non-alcoholic drinks. The alcohol sub-sector includes the distilling of ethyl alcohol, the distilling and blending of spirits and the brewing of wines, cider and beer. The soft drinks sub-sector comprises the processing and bottling of juices, carbonated drinks, natural spring water and mineral water. According to a 2009 survey of manufacturing firms by the National Bureau of Statistics, there are 37 large and medium-sized establishments in the sector, of which 10 are foreign-owned and seven are owned jointly by Tanzanian and foreign investors. Some 15 firms were located in Dar es Salaam, including most of the larger ones. About a third of the firms were established after 2000. The 37 firms together employed a total of 12,593 people and exported goods worth US$2.7 million. Total local sales amounted to US$75 million.

Tanganyika Breweries Ltd, later renamed Tanzania Breweries Ltd (TBL), the country's first brewer, was founded by the colonial government in 1952. The beer business was privatized in the 1990s, and the market opened to other investors. Serengeti Breweries Ltd and Kibo Breweries were founded as locally owned private companies, with East African Breweries of Kenya holding majority shares in the latter. In 2002 East African Breweries agreed with SAB Miller to swap 20% shares in their companies, close down the Kibo Breweries in Moshi and collaborate in the production and distribution of certain brands. (The purpose being to manage the cut-throat competition between the two rivals.) The Diageo group, which has a majority stake in East African Breweries, acquired a majority stake in Serengeti Breweries in 2011. The collaboration between East African Breweries and Serengeti Breweries was therefore terminated, and the two brewers have again become rivals. East African Breweries disposed of its shares in TBL through the Dar es Salaam Stock Exchange in 2011.

In the soft drinks area, the first entrants, who remain dominant in the sector, were franchisees of Coca-Cola and PepsiCo. The first soft drink

TABLE 7.1. Alcoholic beverage production: 2006–10.

	2006	2007	2008	2009	2010
Beer (millions of litres)	299	231	291	285	243
Konyagi (millions of litres)	5	6	4	10	11
Kibuku (millions of litres)	12	10	10	16	21

Source: Tanzania in Figures, National Bureau of Statistics (2011).

bottling plant was set up in 1952 when Greek businessman Aris Cassolis established Tanganyika Bottlers Limited to make Coca-Cola products. Renamed as Tanzania Bottlers in 1964, it was bought by the Mac Group in 1986. The business remained in private hands during the socialist period. In 1995 the South African Bottling Company bought Tanzania Bottlers from Mac Group. SBC Tanzania, a producer of Pepsi soft drinks, began its operations in 2001.

In the juices sub-sector, a number of government-owned processors were established in the 1970s. These ventures were already in financial distress at the time when they were privatized. Subsequently, a number of new private firms entered the sector, using concentrates to make juices. Only recently has one firm, Bakhresa Food Products, begun making juices from fresh fruit as opposed to concentrates.

Bonite Bottlers Ltd was the first Tanzanian company to bottle mineral water; it began its operations in 1990. Several firms entered the market later; these included both small and large firms, and some PepsiCo and Coca-Cola franchisees.

Major sub-sectors of the beverage sector.

Beer and spirits. Tanzania Breweries Ltd operates three plants; Serengeti Breweries operates two. They produce local beers as well as multinational brands, particularly those of their foreign shareholders. Beer and spirits are also produced on a very small scale by informal producers.

Informal spirit production is illegal and informal beer production from grains or banana is restricted to rural or peri-urban localities. The use of poor brewing techniques involving uncontrolled fermentation, unsanitary conditions and the use of rudimentary equipment for processing, packaging and storage results in low-quality products with a short shelf-life.

The production levels for alcoholic beverages are shown in Table 7.1.

Wines. In the 1970s an attempt was made to develop a wine industry, with the establishment of vineyards and a winery in Dodoma. This state-owned company earned a number of international awards for quality, but became

TABLE 7.2. Production of soft drinks: 2004–9.

	2004	2005	2006	2007	2008	2009
Soft drinks (thousands of litres)	264,145	292,878	382,572	450,377	325,277	396,145

Source: National Bureau of Statistics (2010): Statistical Abstract.

financially distressed. The wine industry is now fragmented, with a number of new small producers attempting to compete with imports. The market is small and is restricted to urban areas. Current players include the formerly state-owned Dodoma Wine Limited (now privatized) and a number of small wineries, some of which are owned by missionaries.

Banana alcoholic beverage. Over the past 20 years a new sub-sector has emerged, involving the processing of banana juice into a potent alcoholic beverage. This process was pioneered by Banana Investments of Arusha. The low price of this product drives demand from those of low income, who typically buy traditional beers and spirits produced informally.

Carbonated soft drinks. Aome Tanzanian firms have recently begun to produce local brands. The most prominent of these are Azam Cola, produced by Bakhresa Food Products, and Sayona Cola, produced by Sayona Drinks (part of Motisun Holdings).

Fruit juices. Following the collapse of the government-owned juice processing companies in the 1980s, industrial fruit juices were largely imported, mostly from brand-name multinationals. Until recently, domestic production met only 8% of demand. However, this is changing, in large part due to the recent entry of the Bakhresa group into large-scale fruit juice processing. The juices available in Tanzania include orange, guava, coco-pine, peach, tropical plum and passion fruit.

Bottled water. Bottled water is produced by Coca-Cola and PepsiCo franchisees as well as by large, medium and small-sized local companies. The larger local firms include Sayona Drinks and Bakhresa Food Products.
    The overall volume of production of soft drinks is shown in Table 7.2.

Supply and marketing chain. Malt is produced locally from wheat and sorghum. The beer companies are increasingly entering into outsourcing contracts with local merchants, who collect from smallholders. More recently, Tanzania Breweries, the largest brewer, has been developing contracts with small and medium-sized groups of farmers.

Some beverage companies have their own farms, some maintain supply contracts with individual farmers or groups of farmers, and others buy from merchants who collect produce from small farmers. Many beverage companies use a combination of these strategies. Some inputs—such as corn starch, cans, malt, bottles and barley—are imported because local supply does not meet demand. Due to unreliable supply and long lead times, beverage processors keep large inventories of imported inputs.

Products are distributed via distribution centres, wholesalers and retailers. Some producers deliver directly to retail stores, and some small enterprises deliver directly to the consumers. A small volume of beverages are exported to Kenya, Malawi, Zambia, Mozambique, Burundi, Rwanda, Uganda and the Democratic Republic of the Congo.

Profiles and lines of business of large firms.

Tanzania Breweries Limited, the country's largest brewer, is part of SAB Miller Africa. Its subsidiaries include Tanzania Distilleries Limited and Mountainside Farms Limited. It is engaged in the production, distribution and sale of malt beer, wines and spirits, and alcoholic fruit beverages. It operates breweries in Dar es Salaam, Arusha, Mbeya and Mwanza and produces malt at its malting plant in Moshi. It employs more than 1,400 people.

Serengeti Breweries Limited (SBL) was established as Associated Breweries in 1988, changing its name to Serengeti Breweries in 2002. It produces mild and strong beers as well as energy drinks. With plants in Dar es Salaam and Mwanza, it had a turnover of US$125 million in 2010, employing more than 600 people. A third plant is under construction in Moshi; when it is completed it will boost production by 50%. SBL exports beer to Kenya, Uganda, Rwanda, Burundi, the Democratic Republic of the Congo, the UK and Australia.

Bonite Bottlers Limited, a subsidiary of the IPP Group of Companies, is Tanzania's leading producer of bottled water, selling under its own brand: Kilimanjaro Drinking Water. It also bottles and distributes 12 Coca-Cola brands. Its main plant is located in Moshi. Bonite Bottlers Limited has over 450 permanent employees.

SBC Tanzania Limited, incorporated in 2001, produces and markets PepsiCo's soft drinks under license: Pepsi, Mirinda, Mountain Dew and Seven Up. It employs more than 1,000 people and has a turnover of over US$93 million.

Bakhresa Food Products Limited was established by the Bakhresa group in 1998. It is based in Dar es Salaam and produces eight types of fruit juice and bottled water. Its fruit juice processing plant is the first aseptic packing facility for fruit juices in Tanzania, with a capacity of 41 million litres per annum. It has over 1,000 employees. The company is profiled in Chapter 2.

A-One Products and Bottlers Ltd is part of Mohamed Enterprises Tanzania Ltd (see Chapter 2). It began operations in 1997 in Tanga and was relocated to Dar es Salaam in 1998. It is the group's third largest factory and primarily produces packing materials and beverages. A-One has a strong presence in the market; its brands include Masafi, Just Chill bottled water and Pride juices. The company employs over 1,100 people. A-One plans to establish a second manufacturing division on the shores of Lake Victoria in Mwanza.

Sayona Drinks Ltd is part of the Motisun Holding Group and was the first Tanzanian firm to produce carbonated soft drinks in plastic bottles. It produces cola soda, orange soda, lemon soda and mango juice. The company is exploring export possibilities in Kenya, Mozambique and Uganda. It employs about 320 people, and this total is expected to rise to over 400 in the near future.

Banana Investments Ltd, established in 1993, is the leading producer and distributor of banana-based alcoholic beverages in East Africa. The company has an annual turnover of over US$4 million. Banana Investments employs more than 200 people and has established itself as a significant wholesale buyer for banana growers in Northern Tanzania. The company is now in the process of widening its product range to spirits and bottled water.

Coca-Cola Kwanza Limited is Tanzania's largest bottler of soft drinks, accounting for 40% of the market for carbonated drinks and bottled water. Its turnover in 2010 was around US$70 million. Coca-Cola Kwanza operates ultra-modern plants in Dar es Salaam, Mbeya and Zanzibar.

Profiles and lines of business of medium-sized firms.

Dabaga Vegetables and Fruit Canning Company Ltd, located in Iringa, was for many years the country's sole producer of fresh vegetable products. Its main products are passion fruit and pineapple juices.

Dubai Refreshments and Beverages Limited, located in Mbezi Beach, Dar es Salaam, produces fresh fruit juices from mango and other fruits. Its flagship product is the Maaza brand of mango juice.

TABLE 7.3. Selected small and medium-sized producers of soft drinks.

Company	Location	Main products
Natural Choice	Tanga	Bottled water
Boma la Ngombe Village Ltd	Moshi	Pear juice
All Pack Ltd	Moshi	Spirits
Vegetable Oil Industries Ltd	Mwanza	Bottled water
Tanza Thai IR Ltd	Iringa	Mineral water
Acqua Cool	Dar es Salaam	Bottled Water
K-Cool Water Tanzania Ltd	Dar es Salaam	Drinking water
Just Water Ltd	Arusha	Bottled Water

Some other small and medium-sized companies with products that have been certified by the Tanzania Bureau of Standards are shown in Table 7.3.

Challenges. The challenges facing the industry include the following.

- It is difficult for producers to source consistent volumes and quantities of oranges, wheat, bananas, mangoes and pineapples.
- Shortcomings in water supply from municipal sources have forced many beverage processors to establish their own water sources by drilling boreholes and installing purification plants, adding to their production costs.
- Shortcomings in the railway system forces manufacturers and distributors to rely on road transport, which is costly and congested.
- Erratic power supply has forced producers to rely on costly generators.
- The high and unstable prices of fuel and raw materials significantly increase production costs.

Policy context. Food processing (including beverages) is now a priority sector for the government following the adoption of the Kilimo Kwanza (Agriculture First) resolution.

Recent developments. Some of the larger processors have been developing relationships with small-scale producers. For example, Tanzania Breweries has signed a long-term contract with the glass manufacturer Kioo Limited to procure its bottle requirements. This has enabled Kioo to invest heavily to ensure a sufficient supply of consistent quality to the brewery. Tanzania Breweries is developing contractual relationships with a network of sorghum farmers. Bakhresa Food Products is exploring the possibility of establishing new contract farming arrangements in the Mbeya region.

Beer labels are now produced by Nampak Tanzania Ltd, a local company. Some manufacturers of soft drinks make their own packaging materials or source from sister companies.

7.2   Profiles of Major Firms

7.2.1   Tanzania Breweries Limited (TBL)

Basic details.   TBL is the oldest and largest brewer in Tanzania. Its 2010 turnover was in excess of US$400 million and it employs more than 1,400 people. The company is headquartered in Dar es Salaam and operates four breweries in Mwanza, Mbeya, Kilimanjaro and Arusha. It was one of the first companies to be listed on the Dar es Salaam Stock Exchange.

History.   TBL was established in 1930 as a plant of East African Breweries Limited, then based in Kenya. In March 1960, it was incorporated into Tanganyika Breweries Limited, and in 1964 it was renamed Tanzania Breweries Limited. TBL was nationalized in 1967. Kilimanjaro Breweries Ltd of Arusha was simultaneously consolidated into TBL. The company was privatized in 1993 by the sale of 50% by the government to SAB Miller Africa, with 5% being sold to the International Finance Corporation. In 1998 the company went public, with the remaining government stake being offered to the public. In 2002, 20% of TBL's shares were transferred to East Africa Breweries Limited, a transaction that allowed TBL to acquire the East Africa Breweries operation in Mosho: Kibo Breweries Ltd. In 2010, SAB Miller held 52.87% of the company's shares, East Africa Breweries held 20%, the International Finance Corporation held 3.81%, the government held 4% and the public, including local institutional investors, held the remainder.

Current activities and products.   TBL's main beer brands include Kilimanjaro Premium Lager, Safari Lager, Balimi Extra Lager, Ndovu Special Malt, Bia Bingwa, Redd's Original, Eagle Lager, Miller Genuine Draft, Castle Lager and Castle Milk Stout. Its non-alcoholic beverages include Safari Sparkling Water, Grand Malt and Maltiza Apple. The company has a stake in Tanzania Distilleries Limited, which it manages.

Organization and management.   The managing director, who is a South African national, reports to the firm's board of directors. The management team comprises a mix of Tanzanian and expatriate executives who head divisions of finance, marketing, human resources, sales and distribution, corporate affairs and legal, together with a technical director and the managing director of Tanzania Distilleries Limited.

Firm capabilities. TBL's manufacturing, management and marketing systems draw heavily on the experience of SAB Miller. (SAB Miller was formed from the amalgamation of South African Breweries and the leading American beer maker Miller.) In 2010 TBL opened a new manufacturing plant in Mbeya from which it began exporting beer to Zambia.

Some of the company's brands have won awards, both in South Africa and internationally.

Supply and marketing chain. Most raw materials are sourced locally from farmers and wholesale merchants. For several years TBL faced difficulties in getting reliable supplies of quality bottles. In 2001 it entered into a long-term agreement with Kioo Limited, a local bottle producer, enabling Kioo to make the necessary investments to upgrade its quality. Crown corks are now made locally by Nampak Tanzania Ltd, and labels are produced by Tanzania Printers Ltd. The beer is sold through distribution agents, who act as wholesalers, selling to sub-wholesalers, who in turn sell to retailers across the country.

Exports. TBL exports to the Democratic Republic of the Congo, South Sudan, Kenya, Rwanda, Burundi, Uganda and occasionally to Zambia.

Recent developments. TBL has begun work on protecting water resources, by reducing the amount of water used per litre of beer made (to 4.5 litres of water per litre of beer).

TBL has recently launched a number of new beer brands aimed at low-income consumers.

TBL operates a programme that facilitates the supply of clean and safe water to local communities and institutions.

Development agenda. TBL plans to increase local sourcing, in part via initiatives to promote barley and sorghum farming among the farming community. It also plans to further develop its export activity.

7.2.2   Coca-Cola Kwanza Limited

Basic details. Coca-Cola Kwanza is the leading firm in the industry, with a 40% share of the soft drinks market. It produces over a dozen brands and employs more than 1,000 people in its three plants in Dar es Salaam, Mbeya and Zanzibar.

History.   Tanganyika Bottlers, later renamed Tanzania Bottlers, was established in 1952 by a Greek entrepreneur. The firm was sold in the 1970s
to two Tanzanian businessmen, Yogesh Malik and Jalal Jamal. By the
early 1990s the company operated plants in Dar es Salaam, Mbeya (Afri
Bottlers), Tanga (Sykes Bottlers), Mtwara and Zanzibar. In 1995 the South
African Bottling Company bought a majority share in Tanzania Bottlers Ltd,
injecting US$35 million into the company to establish a modern facility in
Dar es Salaam. The company name was changed in 1995 to Kwanza Bottlers,
and in 1997 to Coca-Cola Kwanza. The other shareholders in the company
include the IPP Group of Companies.

Current activities and products.   Coca-Cola Kwanza produces Coca-Cola,
Coke Light, Fanta, Sprite, Dasani and the Krest and Sparletta ranges.

Organization and management.   The company is managed by a country
manager, who reports directly to the board. He is assisted by heads of
marketing and business development, finance, human resources, manufacturing, commercial (coastal) and commercial (inland).
   The management team includes both Tanzanian and expatriate managers.

Firm capabilities.   Coca-Cola Kwanza has won numerous quality awards
within Coca-Cola International.

Supply and marketing chain.   Coca-Cola Kwanza sources most of the concentrates from Coca-Cola International. Other inputs are largely imported.
The company has a sophisticated distribution network, supported by the
company's own fleet of trucks.

7.2.3   SBC Tanzania Limited

Basic details.   SBC Tanzania is the sole franchisee and bottler of the Pepsi-
Cola range of products in Tanzania. It employs over 1,000 people and has
an annual turnover of more than US$93 million.

History.   The Seven-Up Bottling Company PLC was established by the El-
Khalil family in Nigeria in 1960. The family established SBC Tanzania in
2001, as a franchise operation for Pepsi-Cola.
   The company has its headquarters in Dar es Salaam and operates
plants in Mwanza, Arusha and Mbeya. It has distribution depots in Moshi,
Shinyanga, Dodoma, Iringa and Morogoro.

Current activities and products. SBC Tanzania is engaged in the production, distribution and marketing of Pepsi, 7UP, Mirinda, Mountain Dew and Evervess.

Organization and management. The company is managed by a CEO, who reports to the board. He is assisted by heads of human resources, the technical department, quality assurance, internal audit and corporate affairs.

Firm capabilities. SBC Tanzania's plant is among PepsiCo's best plants in Africa in terms of the group's quality measures.

Supply and marketing chain. SBC Tanzania sources its concentrates from Pepsi-Cola International. Other inputs are largely imported. The company has a sophisticated distribution network, with agents, wholesalers and retailers throughout the country.

Recent developments. SBC Tanzania recently added Mountain Dew to its range of PepsiCo products sold in Tanzania.

Development agenda. The company is currently extending the availability of vending machines across various locations.

7.2.4 Banana Investment Limited (BIL)

Basic details. BIL is engaged in the manufacture of banana-based beverages and wines. It has 300 employees and an annual turnover of around US$3 million.

History. BIL was the first company to commercialize a local brew in Tanzania. It was established by a husband and wife team as an informal, backyard business in 1989, and was formally incorporated in 1993. Since then, the business has grown to become a formally structured, staffed and operated business that is now attracting the attention of several international investors. Until 2007 the production processes were largely manual, and the business depended on a large workforce of casual labourers. Since 2008 most operations have been automated, resulting in a halving of the number of employees.

Current activities and products. Bananas are sourced from various parts of the country and processed into a potent alcoholic beverage, Raha, which is bottled and distributed nationally, through the company's depots and agents. The company also produces banana wines under its Meru and Malkia brands.

Organization and management. The founders of the firm act as managing director and deputy managing director. The company has a board of directors and professional managers of finance, human resources, operations and marketing.

Firm capabilities. BIL's current installed capacity is 60 million bottles of banana beverages per year.

Supply and marketing chain. Ripe bananas are collected from farmers by contracted suppliers who deliver to the factory. To ensure a constant supply of ripe bananas the company has recruited an agricultural expert who visits farmers to provide on-site advice.

The final product is distributed by truck to depots in Tanga, Dar es Salaam, Morogoro and Mwanza and to wholesale buyers in other parts of the country. Wholesalers are responsible for recruiting and supplying retailers. The company undertakes regular advertising and promotional campaigns, and its marketing staff call regularly on wholesale and retail customers.

Recent developments. BIL raised a loan of US$800,000 in 2008 to pay for the automation of most of its production processes.

Development agenda. BIL plans to set up a second plant in Morogoro municipality. This will reduce the transport costs to Dar es Salaam, which is becoming the firm's main market. It is now planning to diversify into spirits and bottled water, and has already begun to produce Fiesta Gin.

7.2.5 Bonite Bottlers Limited

Basic details. Bonite Bottlers, part of the IPP Group of Companies, produces Kilimanjaro Drinking Water, the leading bottled water in Tanzania. The company operates in four regions of Northern Tanzania: Kilimanjaro, Arusha, Manyara and Singida. Bonite Bottlers has more than 450 permanent employees, about 300 of whom work at the firm's main plant in lower Moshi.

History. The history of the IPP Group of Companies dates back to the mid 1980s, when Mr Reginald Abraham Mengi, then a senior partner in Coopers & Lybrand, started a small-scale, hand-operated ballpoint pen assembly at his Dar es Salaam residence. The company gradually diversified into other manufacturing activities, including shoe polish, toilet paper, soaps and detergents, and thermos flasks. The company later moved into the services sector, becoming the largest media company in Tanzania, with interests in radio, television and newspapers. The group also has interests in banking and has three companies involved in mining. Tanzania Gem Centre Limited cuts, facets and polishes precious stones (tanzanite, ruby, sapphire, emerald and alexandrite). Tanza Tanzanite Limited mines tanzanite: a precious stone found only in Tanzania. IPP Resources Limited owns 230 concessions and prospects for gold, base metals, gemstones, uranium, nickel and coal.

Organization and management. Mr Reginald Mengi is the executive chairman of the group. Each company in the group, including Bonite Bottlers, is managed by an independent professional management team under a CEO and a board.

Firm capabilities. Kilimanjaro Drinking Water is one of the most successful products developed by a local private company. Over the years the firm has received numerous quality awards, including a President's Manufacturer of the Year Award in the beverage and tobacco industrial sub-sector.

Chapter 8

TOBACCO

8.1 Sector Profile

Background and overview. Tobacco growing was first introduced by the British colonial government in the Tobora region, and its cultivation spread over time to Shinyanga, Rukwa, Mbeya, Singida, Iringa, Ruvuma, Kigoma, Kagera and Morogoro. Initially cultivated in plantations, it also came to be grown by local farmers on a small scale.

Tanzania produces two varieties of tobacco: some 95% of the crop is Virginia flue cured, while dark fire cured accounts for the remaining 5%.

After independence, the Tobacco Authority of Tanzania was established. It is responsible for tobacco development schemes, infrastructure and extension services, and runs the tobacco research institute. It organizes the chain of activities from buying cured leaf from growers, to keeping individual and village records of inputs, credits and sales, to managing transport, storage, grading, bailing, reprocessing and selling. In 1984 the Tobacco Authority of Tanzania was renamed as the Tanzania Tobacco Processing and Marketing Board.

In 1994/95 most of the processing facilities and infrastructure were privatized. In 2001 the Tanzania Tobacco Processing and Marketing Board was transformed into a regulatory body for the privatized industry; it was renamed the Tanzania Tobacco Board (TTB).

Tobacco production in Tanzania. The tobacco industry in Tanzania is dominated by smallholders and engages over 130,000 families, each growing on an average area of one hectare. It is estimated that the industry provides employment, directly or indirectly, for about 500,000 people (including the field marketing of unprocessed tobacco, tobacco processing and cigarette manufacturing).

Smallholders are organized into 350 primary cooperative societies, which are affiliated to seven secondary (regional) cooperative unions, which are in turn affiliated to the Apex cooperative body.

TABLE 8.1. Trend of tobacco production in Tanzania.

Crop season	Virginia flue cured (mt)	Dark fire cured (mt)	Total (mt)
2001/02	23,084.97	4,812.11	27,897.08
2002/03	30,124.48	3,422.45	33,546.93
2003/04	41,393.00	5,982.99	47,375.99
2004/05	50,494.38	5,228.18	55,722.56
2005/06	46,728.65	3,536.83	50,265.48
2006/07	49,575.93	1,037.97	50,613.9
2007/08	52,596.99	2,474.16	55,071.15
2008/09	55,186.33	3,398.58	58,584.91
2009/10	88,845.13	4,900.76	93,745.89
2010/11	116,000.00	4,400.00	120,400.00

Prior to 2009/10 tobacco production was undertaken through contracts between tobacco buyers and farmers, either on an individual basis or through cooperative societies or farmers' associations. Prices were agreed between farmers' representatives and buyers' representatives in the Tobacco Council (a forum of stakeholders formed to discuss industry issues).

In 2009/10 the government implemented a new system in which cooperatives play a central role. Through their primary societies, farmers source inputs using bank credit. They then sell their cured tobacco to the cooperative societies, who maintain an account with the lending bank. Buyers pay the primary cooperative society through its bank account, and the bank deducts the farmer's loan debt before crediting payments to the primary society account for payment to the farmer. These changes have created better incentives for farmers, and production jumped by 37.5% between 2008/09 and 2009/10 (see Table 8.1 and Figure 8.1).

Tobacco buying and processing. There are three major buyers: Tanzania Leaf Tobacco Company (TLTC), Alliance One Tanzania Ltd (AOTTL) and Premium Active Tanzania Ltd (PATL). AOTTL and TLTC have their own processing facilities, while PATL processes its tobacco using the facilities of its two competitors. Figure 8.2 shows the market shares of the three buyers in 2010.

The two larger buyers, AOTTL and TLTC, organize themselves via the Association of Tanzania Tobacco Traders Ltd. The association deals with the monitoring of the distribution of farming inputs and the provision of agronomic and other technical assistance on behalf of the two companies. This approach helps to reduce operational costs and establish a joint

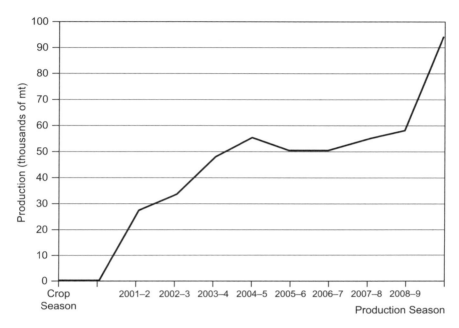

FIGURE 8.1. General trend of tobacco production in Tanzania. Source: TTB.

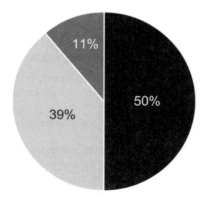

FIGURE 8.2. Market shares of the three major buyers of tobacco in Tanzania. Black: TLTC. Dark grey: PATL. Light grey: AOTTL. Source: Tanzania Tobacco Board and AOTTL.

agronomic approach that address concerns in tobacco cultivation. The Association of Tanzania Tobacco Traders employs about 600 employees and provides agronomy services to over 76,000 small-scale farmers.

The buying process is well organized. Bailed tobacco from farmers is transported to market centres. TTB classifiers inspect samples and assign a grade to each bale. This classification process is witnessed by representatives of the buyers and sellers. A tobacco bale is considered as bought when both representatives are satisfied with the grade assigned.

Upon classification of the bale, a purchase contract note is signed by the buyer's representative and the seller's representative.

Processing and packing of tobacco is done according to the customer's (i.e. the cigarette manufacturer's) specifications or style, which are normally issued well in advance. The specifications will indicate the preferred processing operations, degradation, quality control test requirements, packing moisture, packing weights and packing materials. Most of the Tanzanian tobacco processing facilities can process tobacco in terms of tipping and threshing, loose leaf packing, butted loose leaf and bundles, and hand strips packing.

Regulation.   The TTB was established by Act No. 4 of 1994 to replace the Tanzania Tobacco Processing Marketing Board. The TTB is responsible for licensing tobacco growers and processors. It regulates and enforces quality standards and finances research and development programmes aimed at improving the quality of seeds.

The TTB has established the Tanzania Tobacco Council, whose membership includes tobacco growers represented by primary cooperative societies, tobacco buyers, and representatives from the Ministry of Agriculture. The Tanzania Tobacco Council is a forum for discussing issues such as contractual terms, prices, tobacco grades, loans, the distribution of inputs, and extension services.

Supply chain.   Figure 8.3 shows the tobacco supply chain.

Export status and potential.   Tobacco exports have been growing; the export value in 2010 was US$232.4 million, compared with US$127 million in 2006 (Table 8.2). The major export markets are the Netherlands, Germany and Belgium. The TTB expects exports to grow by about 25% over the next three years, due to increased yield in growing areas.

Profiles and lines of business of large firms.   The main buyers of tobacco are listed below.

Tanzania Leaf Tobacco Company is a subsidiary of the US company Universal Leaf Corporation. The company accounts for a 50% share of the market for processed tobacco.

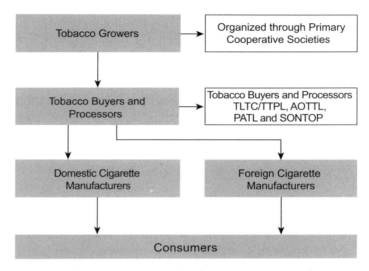

FIGURE 8.3. The tobacco industry supply chain. Source: Annual Report, Ministry of Agriculture and Food Security (2011).

TABLE 8.2. Trends in tobacco exports in Tanzania.

Year	Forex-earned (millions of US$)
2005	176.4
2006	127.4
2007	232.4
2010	232.4

Source: Annual Report, Ministry of Agriculture and Food Security (2011).

Alliance One Tobacco Tanzania Ltd, also profiled below, is an affiliate of the US multinational Alliance One International. AOTTL has its headquarters in Morogoro and accounts for a 39% share of the market for processed tobacco.

Premium Active Tanzania Ltd, an affiliate of Premium Holdings International, accounts for about 11% of the market for processed tobacco. This is the only major buyer that does not have its own processing facilities.

Songea Tobacco Processors is owned by farmers through their cooperative societies and union. Their plant had an annual processing capacity of 13 million kg, but it is not currently operational. Efforts are underway to upgrade the facility.

Tanzania Cigarette Company Ltd (TCCL), profiled below, is a subsidiary of the Japan Tobacco International group of companies, which owns 75% of its shares. The remaining shares are traded on the Dar es Salaam Stock Exchange.

Mastermind Tobacco (T) Ltd is a subsidiary of the Mastermind group of companies, which has manufacturing plants in Kenya, Uganda, the Democratic Republic of the Congo, Burundi, Angola and South Africa. Mastermind Tobacco (T) was incorporated in 1996 and it produces four brands of cigarettes. The company has a very small market share (less than 1%).

Challenges. A substantial challenge to the sector is that infrastructure is inadequate to cope with growing production. Tobacco stakeholders are being urged to invest in facilities such as tobacco curing barns, market centres/godowns, the rural road network and primary processing facilities.

The inadequate provision of extension services is hampering the sector, and the TTB is now mobilizing industry stakeholders through public–private partnership initiatives to improve these services.

Rationale for selecting profiled firms. AOTTL and TCCL are both among the leading firms in the industry.

8.2 Profiles of Major Firms

8.2.1 *Alliance One Tobacco Tanzania Ltd*

Basic details. AOTTL is involved in buying, processing and selling tobacco to local and international cigarette manufacturers. Headquartered in Morogoro municipality, it has 280 permanent employees and about 2,000 seasonal employees. Turnover in 2010 was about US$103 million, of which about 95% came from exports.

History. AOTTL was established in 2005 following a worldwide merger between DIMON Incorporated and the Standard Commercial Corporation, both from the US. Prior to the merger, both companies had already been operating in the Tanzanian Tobacco industry. The Standard Commercial Corporation began its operations in Tanzania in the early 1960s and DIMON came to Tanzania in 1995.

Current activities and products. AOTTL buys over 30 million kg of tobacco per annum from more than 160 contracted Farmers' Cooperative Primary Societies, spread over seven tobacco-growing regions. The firm has a modern tobacco processing facility, with a processing capacity of 60 million kg per annum.

The facility can process tobacco via topping and threshing, total threshing, loose leaf packing, butted loose leaf and bundles, and hand strips packing.

Organization and management. AOTTL's board of directors is chaired by the managing director, who is also the CEO. The company has four divisions: leaf, sales, factory and finance, and human resources.

Firm capabilities. The firm accounts for 39% of tobacco sales in Tanzania. It has a state-of-the-art processing facility and has established strong relationships with some 39,000 farmers who produce organic and high-quality tobacco.

Supply and marketing chain. Leaf tobaccos are bought at an agreed price set by the Tanzania Tobacco Council. Bailed classified tobaccos are bought at market centres from farmers or primary cooperative societies. The processed tobacco is sold to both local and foreign cigarette manufacturers.

Exports. AOTTL exports over 95% of its output. The value of its exports in 2010 was about US$90 million.

Development agenda. The company expanded its processing capacity from 35,000 mt per annum to 50,000 mt per annum in 2011, and plans a further expansion to 60,000 mt per annum by 2014.

A recent US$10 million project involved the introduction of a computerized system of loading and receiving tobacco, aimed at reducing handling time and green leaf storage at the factory.

The firm encourages environmentally friendly farming, and is helping tobacco farmers to be self-sufficient in wood fuel supply, both for tobacco curing and for domestic use, through a reforestation programme.

8.2.2   Tanzania Cigarette Company Ltd

Basic details. TCCL is a subsidiary of the Japan Tobacco International group of companies. It provides direct employment to over 650 Tanzanians and indirectly supports over 85,000 tobacco farmers and over 2,500 distributors, retailers and suppliers. The firm's turnover in 2010 was more than US$230 million.

History. TCCL was established in 1961 as a subsidiary of East African Tobacco Ltd of Kenya, and it was nationalized in 1967. The company was then privatized in 1995, and was acquired by R. J. Reynolds of the US. R. J. Reynolds and its stake in TCCL were in turn acquired in 1999 by Japan Tobacco International, an international arm of Japan Tobacco, the world's third largest tobacco company. In November 2000 TCCL was listed on the Dar es Salaam Stock Exchange. Japan Tobacco International holds over 75% of the shares of TCCL.

Current activities and products. The company produces cigarettes for sale on both the domestic and regional markets. Its brands include Camel, LD, Embassy, Iceberg, Monte Carlo, Sweet Menthol, Safari, Club, Aspen and Crescent Star.

Organization and management. The board of directors of TCCL consists of seven directors, four of whom hold executive positions in the company. The general manager oversees departments of finance, manufacturing, the East and Central Africa division, human resources, company services, legal, corporate affairs, and consumer and trade marketing.

Firm capabilities. TCCL is the only domestic producer of cigarettes and accounts for 90% of cigarette sales. It is among the top 10 tax payers in the country. TCCL derives its capabilities from adoption of the parent company's global standards, policies and procedures and operating guidelines. The firm's production facilities meet international quality standards and it is ISO certified.

Supply and marketing chain. TCCL sources its inputs from domestic processors of tobacco. The firm's distribution channels are well established, having been developed over the past four decades.

Exports. TCCL exports to the Democratic Republic of the Congo, Mozambique, Malawi, Zambia and Comoros. Its export revenue in 2010 was US$15 million, or some 6% of the firm's total sales revenue.

Development agenda. TCCL plans to expand its production capacity and expand its sales to other countries in the region.

Chapter 9

SUGAR

9.1 Sector Profile

Background and overview. The sugar industry directly 17,500 people employs and provides a livelihood to some 18,500 small-scale cane out-growers.[1] It accounts for 35% of the gross output by volume of food manufacturing and 8.5% of total value-added in manufacturing. Sugar output, however, provides only 75% of Tanzania's consumption, with the remaining 25% of consumption being met by imports.[2]

There are four major sugar companies in the country: Kagera Sugar Limited (KSL), Tanganyika Planting Company (TPC), Kilombero Sugar Company (KSC), with two sugarcane estates and two factories, and Mtibwa Sugar Estate (MSE), which owns both estates and a factory. There are also a number of very small producers, whose activities are described below (Table 9.1).

Sugar production began in early 1930 when TPC began producing granular sugar at a small plant at Arusha Chini. Larger-scale production began in 1936 with a crushing capacity of 350 mt per day. The 1940–60 period saw an expansion of the TPC plant to a capacity of 1,500 mt per day, and the installation of three additional small plants at Karangai in Arusha, Bukoba (Kagera) and Turiani (Mtibwa).

The first large sugar project in Tanzania after independence, Kilombero I, began as a sugarcane out-growers programme. Another out-grower programme formed the basis of the Mtibwa project.

The Sugar Development Corporation (SDC) was established under the Public Corporation Act of 1964 to promote the development of the industry. Production increased steadily from an annual average of 49,000 mt between 1961 and 1965 to an annual average of 115,200 mt during the period 1976–80. The volume of cane grown by out-growers increased from an annual

---

[1] Sugar Board of Tanzania. 2009. *Annual Report, 2008/09.*

[2] Rothe, A., K. Görg and Y. Zimmer. 2007. The future competitiveness of sugar beet production in the EU in comparison to sugar cane production in developing countries. Report, Federal Agriculture Research Centre.

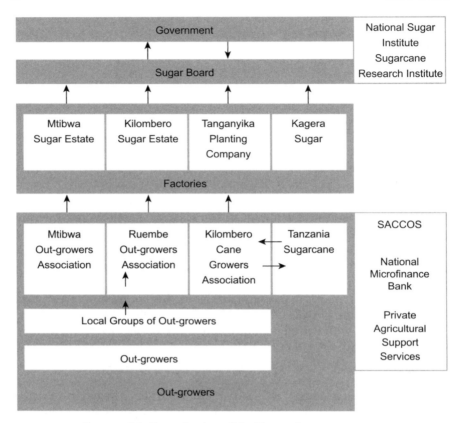

FIGURE 9.1. Organization of the Tanzanian sugar sector.

average of 17,552 mt between 1961 and 1965 to an average of 157,000 mt between 1981 and 1985.

However, in 1967 (when all factories were nationalized) production declined to around 99,000 mt. This period also saw a drastic decline in cane production by out-growers.

Nationalization ended in 1986, with privatization and restructuring of the industry. The SDC was restructured as the Sugar Board of Tanzania (SBT) and was made responsible for the regulation, coordination and development of the industry. Following privatization, production rose from 135,535 mt in 2001 to 263,461 mt in 2010. However, production falls far short of demand, and shortages have led to substantial price rises. The government has responded by allowing private companies to import duty-free sugar for the fiscal year ending June 2012.

Sugarcane is grown both by the major companies and by private out-growers. Out-growers are represented by four associations: the Ruembe Cane Growers Association, the Kilombero Cane Growers Association, the Mtibwa Out-growers Association and the Kagera Sugarcane Growers Association. The Tanzanian Sugar Cane Growers Association is the national representative of cane growers.

The Sugar Cane Research Institute in Kibaha carries out trials and research in pest and disease control, and in agronomic improvements. The National Sugar Institute in Kidatu provides training for growers and owners of sugar processing plants. The National Microfinance Bank and the Savings and Credit Cooperative Organization provide microcredit to out-growers. The Private Agricultural Support Service provides support in the form of financial services (access to finance) and business development services (feasibility studies, business plans and market linkages) to out-growers.

Supply and marketing chain. Sugarcane transportation is managed through contracts between sugar factories and private trucking companies. Sugar is transported by road to centres of consumption. Molasses are sold to the interested companies and wholesalers. Baggase is burnt to produce power (electricity); most is used directly by the sugar companies and a small amount is sold to the national grid (Figure 9.1).

Challenges. Current problems facing the industry include the following.

- Sugarcane ratoon stunting disease can cause cane yield reductions of over 50% through stunted growth and reductions in plant population.
- Monovariety of NCO 376 in estate and out-grower cane fields. This variety occupies 96% of estate cane fields and 100% of out-grower cane fields. The variety, though high yielding, is highly susceptible to smut and ratoon stunting disease.
- Low irrigation efficiency (below 75%) arising from inadequate density of pipes and sprinklers. Water storage facilities are in many cases inadequate.
- Low skill levels and low levels of training among out-growers.
- A lack of irrigation facilities on out-grower land can force out-growers to rely wholly on rain-fed cane.
- The high input costs of fertilizer and herbicides.
- Poor infrastructure in out-grower areas, which hinders the transportation of harvested cane to factories and can result in poor cane quality, as cane is stale on arrival, leading to losses.
- The importation of illegal sugar from Malawi and Zambia.

TABLE 9.1. Sugar production by the four major factories, 2001–10 (mt).

Year	KSC	TPC	MSE	KSL	Total
2001	61,688	42,018	31,829	0	135,535
2002	72,499	49,681	41,151	0	163,188
2003	98,420	54,850	36,850	0	190,120
2004	12,674	62,519	34,577	0	223,788
2005	126,253	52,756	35,081	15,400	229,863
2006	136,944	60,503	49,170	16,703	263,317
2007	103,681	34,887	33,666	19,678	192,003
2008	127,432	59,247	44,802	33,951	265,434
2009	118,026	78,483	42,863	40,482	279,851
2010	119,623	68,616	40,029	35,193	263,461

Source: SBT (2010).

Profiles and lines of business of large firms.   The four major producers are as follows.

Kilombero Sugar Company Limited produces approximately 42% of total output. It is profiled in the next section.

Tanganyika Planting Company Limited produces approximately 25% of sugarcane output. It is profiled in the next section.

Mtibwa Sugar Estate Ltd. is part of Tanzania Sugar Industries Limited, which is owned by a consortium of Tanzanian business people. Cane is mostly supplied from the company's own fields in Morogoro, with a small portion coming from small out-growers in surrounding villages. MSE contracts smallholder farmers who are members of the Mtibwa Out-growers Association. The relationship between the Mtibwa Out-growers Association and MSE is defined by the Sugar Industry Act (2001), under which the SBT regulates the industry. Before the harvesting season, MSE and the Mtibwa Out-growers Association agree terms. MSE produces sugar, bio-energy, animal feeds, fertilizers and ethanol. It produces 40,000 mt of sugar per annum. Some of this output is exported to the EU under the Africa Caribbean Pacific–EU sugar protocol, while the rest is sold locally.

Kagera Sugar Limited, on being privatized in December 2001, became a member of the Super group of companies. It is located in the northwestern part of Tanzania (close to the Tanzania–Uganda border). KSL takes advantage of its location on the River Kagera, which provides a source of water for irrigation. KSL has invested heavily in its centre-pivot irrigation system, its high-tech reel irrigators and its overhead sprinklers. Its current capacity is approximately 35,000 mt of sugar per annum.

TABLE 9.2. Sugarcane production by out-growers.

| Company location | 2009/10 & 2008/09 | | | | Number of cane out-growers | |
| | Hectares | | Cane (mt) | | | |
	2008/09	2009/10	2008/09	2009/10	2008/09	2009/10
Kilombero	11,200	13,106	473,457	413,640	12,255	8,557
Mtibwa	8,692	1,100	216,600	179,884	5,800	4,527
Kagera	113	235	2,712	4,082	326	326
Total	20,005	24,341	692,769	597,606	18,381	13,410

Source: SBT (2010).

Small-scale sugar producers.   There are four types of small-scale production.

• There are two mini plants in the country: at Wami Prison and at Dudumera in Babati district. Between them they are capable of producing 1,000–2,000 mt of sugar per annum.

• There are 13 village-level sugar plants in the country, with a capacity to crush about 2.5 mt of cane per hour, producing 100–600 kg of sugar per day.

• Household-level sugar producers crush cane using manual or electrical cane crushers. The operations involve juice extraction using sugarcane crushers, concentration of the sugarcane juice by boiling it on an open fire, crystallization of the resulting syrup and then separation of the sugar crystals from the molasses by gravitation drainage. The sugar is finally sun dried.

• It is estimated that there are about 22 producers of jaggery in the country, operating on a total area of about 5,000 hectares, who produce over 20,000 mt of jaggery per annum. Jaggery is a traditional unrefined whole cane sugar. It is a concentrated product of cane juice, without separation of molasses and crystals, and can vary from golden brown to dark brown in colour. Jaggery can complement or substitute for granular sugar.

Sugarcane out-growers.   Sugarcane out-growers operate on a total of about 24,000 hectares at Kilombero, Mtibwa and Kagera. They provide over 40% of total cane supply to the factories in their areas (see Tables 9.2 and 9.3).

Rationale for selecting profiled firms. The two profiled firms are leading firms in terms of production levels, employment and the size of their estates. While KSC engages sugarcane out-growers, TPC does not.

9.2   Profiles of Major Firms

9.2.1   Kilombero Sugar Company limited

Basic details. KSC is 55% owned by Illovo Sugar Limited of South Africa. The government of Tanzania owns 25% and ED&F Man Holdings Limited, a company based in the UK, owns 20%. The headquarters and operations of KSC are in the Kilombero valley, which is divided into two districts: Kilombero and Kilosa. It is the largest sugar-processing company in Tanzania, processing two types of sugar at two factories: one in Msolwa (Kilombero 1, or K1) and one in Ruhembe (Kilombero 2, or K2). K1 produces brown sugar, while K2 is the only factory in Tanzania that produces refined white sugar. KSC processes over 120,000 mt of sugar per annum. The company has 850 permanent employees and 1,900 seasonal agricultural workers. During the peak season it employs up to 4,500 workers.

History. KSC was incorporated on 30 May 1960 in what was then called Tanganyika and it established the out-growers associations in 1961. The original factory at Msolwa (K1) was built in 1962 by private investors. In 1968 the government bought all the shares in the company from the initial investors. In 1972 these shares were entrusted to the National Agriculture and Food Corporation, and then to the SDC when it was formed in 1974. The second factory, at Ruembe (K2), was built in 1976.

   The company was privatized in April 1998, leading to the current pattern of shareholding. After privatization, Illovo Sugar Limited invested US$50 million into the rehabilitation of the K2 factory. A further US$3.5 million was invested later.

   In 2004 a refinery was installed, at a cost of US$5.5 million and with an annual production capacity of 65,000 mt of refined sugar. From 2003 to 2005 KSC, with the support of International Finance Cooperation, established Kilombero Community Trust. Kilombero Community Trust supports the farming community to obtain loans, both for sugarcane development and for other crops. Annual production has increased from 29,000 mt in the year before privatization to the current level of 120,000 mt.

Current activities and products. KSC's main products are sugar, molasses and bagasse for use in boilers. Kilombero also provides 50 MWh per day

TABLE 9.3. Sugar cane cultivation, 1991/92–2006/07.

Year	KSC			MSE					Total estate	Total O/G	Grand total
	Estate	OG	Total	Estate	OG	Total	TPC	KSL			
1991/92	460,262	97,234	557,496	201,619	77,094	278,713	347,861	86,477	1,096,219	174,328	1,270,547
1992/93	426,736	133,154	559,890	186,149	139,547	325,696	392,703	60,790	1,066,378	272,701	1,339,079
1993/94	488,764	158,042	646,806	161,511	325,696	487,207	397,850	56,974	1,105,099	483,738	1,588,837
1994/95	416,418	178,500	594,918	170,608	224,574	395,182	233,350	56,250	876,626	403,074	1,279,700
1995/96	366,059	155,003	521,062	165,648	215,480	381,128	402,575	64,845	999,127	370,483	1,369,610
1996/97	316,696	135,700	452,396	131,064	211,325	342,389	424,531	77,765	950,056	347,025	1,297,081
1997/98	294,436	95,765	390,201	178,168	80,013	258,181	312,056	23,465	808,125	175,778	983,903
1998/99	311,610	133,500	445,110	126,143	209,170	335,313	435,600	43,655	917,008	342,670	1,259,678
1999/00	395,228	109,400	504,628	173,564	172,485	346,049	344,807	—	913,599	281,885	1,195,484
2000/01	418,664	125,130	543,794	220,777	120,144	340,921	447,759	—	1,087,200	245,274	1,332,474
2001/02	429,851	192,979	622,830	202,000	246,143	448,143	451,887	—	1,083,738	439,122	1,522,860
2002/03	584,708	246,529	831,237	251,218	176,000	427,218	552,302	—	1,388,228	422,529	1,810,757
2003/04	665,206	429,632	1,094,838	197,556	240,201	437,757	621,001	—	1,483,763	669,833	2,153,596
2004/05	622,037	588,051	1,210,088	186,525	241,063	427,588	512,944	201,741	1,523,247	829,114	2,352,361
2005/06	524,789	696,253	1,221,042	248,554	259,952	508,505	594,778	177,209	1,545,330	956,205	2,501,534
2006/07	507,774	481,147	988,921	232,122	129,624	361,746	417,894	271,791	1,429,581	610,771	2,040,352

Note: 'OG' denotes outgrowers.
Source: Annual Report 2010, Sugar Board of Tanzania. Ministry of Agriculture and Food Security.

to the regional grid of the Tanzania Electricity Supply Company through co-generation, at a price of around US$0.06 per kWh.

Organization and management. The board comprises members of Illovo Sugar Limited together with two Tanzanians: the director general of SBT and a government treasury official. The top management team are mostly expatriates.

Firm capabilities. KSC's sugar is regarded as the best that is produced in Tanzania. Average cane yield per acre is 78 mt and the average capacity utilization is 76%.

Supply and marketing chain. Sugarcane is grown by out-growers surrounding the mills. KSC offers annually renewable contracts to out-growers. Smallholder farmers' farms are organized by two farmers' associations. The farms supplying sugarcane to K1 belong to the Kilombero Cane Growers Association. Those who supply K2 are located in the Kilosa district and belong to the Ruhembe Out-growers Association. Most of the out-growers grow sugarcane on small farms of between half a hectare and 2 hectares, with very few small-scale farmers having farms of more than 4 hectares. Cane production is dependent on both rain-fed and irrigation agriculture. Much of the water originates from the Udzungwa Mountains.

Lime is locally produced at the Tanga limestone works.

KSC serves the southern regions of Tanzania: Mtwara and the Lindi region by the sea route, and the Mbeya, Ruvuma and Rukwa regions by road. It also serves the Morogoro, Dar es Salaam and Coast regions.

Exports. In the past, KSC exported sugar to the Seychelles, Ruanda and Burundi and to Europe under the Lome Africa Caribbean Pacific–EU sugar protocol. Presently, exports are minimal. There is a small export business around molasses, which is also sold in the domestic market.

Recent developments. The company has recently invested in mobile health clinics and comprehensive infrastructure development for cane haulage.

Development agenda. The management of KSC and Illovo Sugar Limited plan to set up a new plant at Ruipa in the Kilombero valley. There is also a plan to expand existing mills, enabling the company to crush all the cane that is currently being produced by out-growers. An alcohol plant, to produce paper and clipboards from bagasse, is also under consideration. The company plans to undertake improvements in relation to its power supplies.

9.2.2   Tanganyika Planting Company

Basic details.   TPC, the second largest sugar company in Tanzania, has capacity to produce over 650,000 mt of sugar per annum. The company employs 2,667 permanent employees, 591 temporary workers and 636 seasonal workers. The estate is situated 24 km from Moshi, in the Northern region.

History.   TPC was established in the early 1930s by A. P. Mollar, a Danish ship owner operating along the East African coast. Mollar initially acquired land to provide a facility for his ship crews, later establishing a small sugar plant.

The company began to produce sugar in 1936. The estate operated as a branch of A/S Tanganyika Planting Company Limited, registered in Denmark. In the late 1960s the company was nationalized and became a subsidiary of the Sugar Corporation. In 2000 it was privatized, and Sukari Investment Company Limited purchased a 75% stake, with the remaining 25% being held by the Tanzanian government. Sukari Investment Company is registered in Mauritius and is jointly owned by a Mauritian company, Deep River Beau Champ Limited, and a French firm, Sucrière de la Réunion.

Current activities and products.   The company grows sugarcane on its own estate using full-time, part-time and seasonal workers, and produces sugar and molasses. Sugarcane is grown entirely under irrigation.

Electricity is generated at the factory premises using steam turbines to burn bagasse (a form of biomass that is a waste material from the pressing of sugarcane). The company generates enough power in this way to fully cover its own requirements, while selling surplus power to the national grid.

The performance of TPC in sugarcane growing and sugar production from 2000/01 to 2008/09 is shown in Table 9.4.

Organization and management.   TPC is currently managed by its Mauritian owner Deep River Bean Champ Ltd. The board of directors, to which the CEO reports, comprises members from both its Mauritian owners and its French owners as well as two members appointed by the Tanzanian government.

Firm capabilities.   The firm benefits from having experienced managers and from the technical knowhow of its Mauritian parent company. Its sugar has a well-established reputation for quality.

Supply and marketing chain.   TPC sells largely to nearby regions: Kilimanjaro, Arusha, Tanga, Manyara, Singida, Mara and Musoma.

TABLE 9.4. Sugarcane and sugar production at TPC 2000/01–2009/10 (mt).

Years	Sugarcane production	Sugar production
2000/01	447,759	42,018
2001/02	451,887	49,681
2002/03	552,302	54,850
2003/04	621,001	62,519
2004/05	521,944	52,756
2005/06	594,778	60,503
2006/07	417,894	34,887
2007/08	699,241	59,247
2008/09	787,766	78,483

Challenges. Cane productivity at TPC is low, in part because of high infestation of the cane root by feeding pests of the white grub complex. These pests not only damage the cane but also increase costs due to the need for frequent replanting. Salinity and high sodium toxicity levels in the soil also contribute to low cane productivity.

Due to poor weather conditions, about 60% of the water supplied for irrigation to TPC is from boreholes, while only 40% is from rivers. Water from boreholes is pumped by diesel and electric pumps and this increases costs.

Other varieties of cane, with high yield potential, are now being introduced on the estate.

Recent developments. Following privatization, TPC invested US$32 million into rehabilitation of its factory, the irrigation system, field equipment, transport and the expansion of the cane fields.

The company received loans from the owners to replace old boilers and turbo alternators, which had been problematic. Additional land acquired during privatization was put under irrigation.

Development agenda. Modernization of the factory and improvement in cane husbandry practices, and the use of higher-yielding disease-resistant cane varieties, are expected to bring TPC to an annual output level of 84,000 mt by 2016–20.

Chapter 10

SISAL

10.1 Sector Profile

Background and overview. Sisal production in Tanzania dates back to 1893, when the first plantations were introduced by Dr Richard Hindorf of the German East Africa Company.

By the 1960s Tanzania had become the world's largest producer of sisal (Brazil, Mexico and Kenya are the next-largest producers). In 1964 annual production stood at 240,000 mt and sisal was being grown on 487,000 hectares of land. Sisal was at that time the country's most important foreign exchange earner, and sisal production was Tanzania's largest industry in terms of employment.

Prior to the Arusha Declaration of 1967, sisal production was wholly in the hands of the private sector. Following the Arusha Declaration, about half of the industry was nationalized. The nationalized estates were managed at first by the Tanzania Sisal Corporation and then, from 1973, by the newly formed Tanzania Sisal Authority. Three companies—Amboni Limited, Ralli Estates Limited and Karimjee Agricultural Limited—remained in private hands; however, the marketing of sisal and its products were under the control of the Tanzania Sisal Authority.

From the 1960s onwards the industry has experienced a steady decline. Output fell from 230,000 mt in 1964 to a low point of 20,489 mt in 2000 (see Figure 10.1).

The development of synthetic fibres in Europe and North America, which accelerated in the 1970s, displaced over 60% of the demand for natural fibres. Few alternative uses for sisal were available, apart from making agricultural twines for hay bailing and making bags. Recent advances in technology have extended the use of sisal to the production of biogas, electricity generation and bio-fertilizers.

Sisal plantations traditionally employ more than 500 people on an estate of between 3,000 and 7,500 hectares and incorporate a primary processing facility. Recently, small-scale sisal farming has been successfully established in the Tanga region by Katani Ltd. The company's Sisal

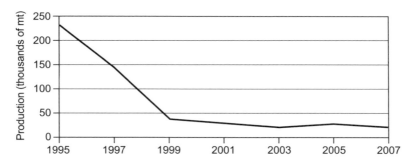

FIGURE 10.1. The trend in sisal production (mt).
Source: Tanzania Sisal Board (2011).

Smallholder and Outgrower scheme involves a form of contract farming that has engaged 2,000 smallholder farmers in the Tanga region, where more than 12,000 hectares of land have been planted. The same scheme is now being extended to the Lake Zone and the Western Zone.

Profiles and lines of business of large firms.   Some 21 sisal estates and six spinning mills now produce fibre products such as twines, sisal bags and ropes.

Katani Ltd is privately owned, vertically integrated company operating in the Tanga region. It accounts for some 30% of industry output. The company operates sisal decortication factories on five estates: Hale, Mwelya, Ngombezi, Magoma and Magunga. The company engages in primary processing, spinning and weaving, producing sisal fibres, ropes, twines, carpets, fine yarns, buffing cloth and geotextiles. Katani also owns Tancord (1998) (the largest spinning and weaving mill in Africa) as well as Mkonge Energy Systems (a sisal energy company with facilities at Hale estate). It is also involved in developing best practices in sisal farming and producing renewable energy from sisal biomass.

D. D. Ruhinda & Co. Ltd was established in 1991 by Mr Damian Ruhinda, who had been the CEO of the Tanganyika Sisal Marketing Board and later of the Ngomeni Sisal Spinning Mill. The company, which is headquartered in Tanga city, started out as a trading house specializing in buying and selling local fibre produce. After becoming well established in trading, the company ventured into the cultivation and decortication of sisal by buying the state-owned Mkumbara Sisal Estates in 1997. The estates have a total area of 1,734 hectares. Current yield stands at 1.8 mt per hectare and the company employs about 280 employees.

China State Farms Agribusiness (Group) Corporation (Tanzania) Limited is a Chinese state-owned firm. It is profiled in the next section.

Sagera Estates Ltd was established in 1996. The company specializes in growing sisal and manufacturing sisal fibres and yarn. The firm has four major estates: Kwarungu, Kwa Mdulu, Lubungo and Amboni. It also has a spinning mill popularly known as Usambara Spinning Mill. The current annual production capacity of the firm stands at over 5,000 mt of fibres and 2,400 mt of yarn.

Mohamed Enterprises (T) Ltd, part of the METL group profiled in Chapter 2, produces and/or adds value to more than 30% of Tanzania's sisal output. The company produces about 8,000 mt of sisal fibres per annum from its six estates located in the Tanga and Coast regions. Most of the sisal produced on its 10,000 hectares of estates is processed by Tanzania Packing Materials (1998) and 21st Century Holdings (two other METL subsidiaries: see below).

Tanzania Packing Materials (1998) Ltd was established in 1998 through the acquisition of two state-owned corporations: Morogoro Bags Manufacturing Company and Moshi Bags Manufacturing Company. Tanzania Packing Materials (1998) produces sisal bags of natural biodegradable fibre that are sold on both the home and export markets. These bags are mainly used for storing agricultural produce. The firm employs about 650 people.

21st Century Holdings Ltd was established in 2001 through acquisition of one of the state-owned sisal spinning corporations in Dar es Salaam. It manufactures a range of sisal yarns for tie ropes and sisal fabrics, and fine yarn for floor covering. Most of the firm's output is exported to Japan, India, Yemen, Spain, Italy, the Netherlands, France and Ethiopia.

Supply and marketing chain.   Most sisal is produced on large estates that have processing facilities for decorticating and drying. Very little is sold to local spinning and weaving mills. Most producers sell through international auctions.

Exports.   Table 10.1 shows sisal exports for 2009 and 2010. (Exports were relatively low in 2009 because of low demand in the world market.) The main export destinations are Europe, China and the Middle East.

Policy context.   The Tanzania Sisal Board, which took over the regulatory role of the former Tanzania Sisal Authority in 1997, is responsible for issuing export and import licenses, for regulation and quality control and for marketing. It also conducts research and development on sisal growing, and on

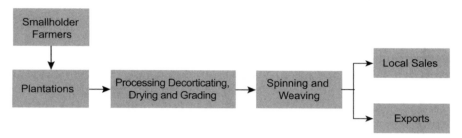

FIGURE 10.2. The sisal supply chain.

TABLE 10.1. Export trend of sisal fibres and products, 2009–10.

Year	Export of sisal fibre (mt)	Export of sisal products (mt)
2009	8,239	5,349
2010	11,558	6,408

Source: Tanzania Sisal Board (2011).

the development of alternative uses for sisal. The United Nations Industrial Development Organization, the Common Fund for Commodities and the Food and Agriculture Organization are also involved in supporting the development of the sisal sector, especially in relation to the use of sisal biomass.

Competitiveness.   Sisal farming is capital intensive and substantial financing is needed to develop estates. Following denationalization in the late 1990s most of the estates were in poor condition. Long-term loans are now needed to rebuild the sector.

Challenges.   High fuel costs are a continuing source of concern, as is weakness in electricity supply. Most firms operate below capacity.

   Tanzania's tax system does not give special treatment to the agricultural sector, and sisal producers face multiple taxes from local authorities.

10.2   Profiles of Major Firms

10.2.1   *D. D. Ruhinda & Co. Ltd*

Basic details.   Established in 1990 by Mr Damian David Ruhinda, the firm's headquarters are in Tanga city and its estate is located at Mkumbara.

D. D. Ruhinda is engaged in the production of sisal fibres. The firm employs about 280 people.

History. Before establishing the firm Mr Ruhinda worked as the director of marketing for the Tanzania Sisal Authority (the state authority that managed all sisal estates during the era of the command economy) and subsequently as the managing director of the Tanzania Sisal Marketing Association. Mr Ruhinda's experience in fibre trading enabled him to build credibility with international sisal dealers. In 1990 he established D. D. Ruhinda as a trading house, buying and selling local fibre. After establishing a successful trading operation he then used a combination of personal savings and a bank loan to acquire a sisal estate at Mkumbara that had formerly been state owned. At the time of acquisition the estate was at a standstill, employing only 20 or so staff. By 2000, however, it was employing 80 people.

Current activities and products. The company's main product at present is sisal fibre of various grades.

Organization and management. The managing director, who reports to a board of directors, is responsible for the day-to-day management of the company. He is supported by four heads of department: finance and administration, estates, spinning and engineering.

Firm capabilities. The company is now setting up a sisal spinning mill to produce sisal yarns, twines and buffing cloth. It also has a small production unit for sisal carpets.

Supply and marketing chain. Sisal bulbils are produced in the company's plantation. Sisal is resistant to drought and disease and there is therefore only a modest requirement for imported chemicals and pesticides.

Most sisal fibre is exported but new products such as sisal yarns and twine are sold in the local market. Local sales are mainly large-volume sales to producers of sisal products (weavers).

Exports. The company exports about 80% of its output, predominantly to China and Europe.

Challenges. The firm's main problems relate to its limited access to capital, the irregular nature of its power supplies, the escalating prices for its fuel and the unfavourable tax regime it faces.

Development agenda. The company needs to add more value to its raw sisal in order to improve growth and profitability.

The firm now aims to

- design and install a modern sisal decorticator that uses less water and electricity but produces more sisal per day,
- install a biogas plant to transform sisal waste for biogas, electricity and bio-fertilizer, and
- carry out research and development into the use of sisal fibre for manufacturing building materials (tiles and blocks).

10.2.2   *China State Farms Agribusiness (Group) Corporation (Tanzania) Limited*

Basic details. The company is a Chinese state-owned firm that is engaged in the production of sisal fibre. Its annual turnover is around US$1.5 million, and it employs more than 900 people. The firm operates on 1,218 hectares of land.

History. The company was established in Tanzania in 1999 under the name Zhongken Investment Agribusiness Tanzania Limited. In 2000 the name was changed to China State Farms Agribusiness (Group) Corporation (Tanzania) Limited. The project was attractive because of the availability of abundant fertile land with appropriate infrastructure, and with the Tanzania–Zambia Railway. Production of sisal fibres began in 2004, after a four-year planting period.

Current activities and products. The firm's current output consists wholly of sisal fibres.

Organization and management. The firm has a board of directors and a managing director who is responsible for the daily management of company activities. Members of the board of directors are appointed by the government of the People's Republic of China. The managing director oversees seven departmental heads: operations, agricultural machinery and plant, agricultural economics, finance and administration, estates, security and health.

Firm capabilities. Using advanced agricultural technology, machinery, processes and expertise, the firm achieves the highest yield of sisal fibre per hectare in Tanzania. Due to its Chinese government connections the firm has access to ample financial resources, which have facilitated its expansion, allowing it to plant about 150 hectares per annum over the last four years.

Supply and marketing chain. Sisal bulbils come from the firm's plantation. Chemicals pesticides, spare parts and agricultural machinery are imported from China.

Exports. Initially, the firm sold fibre in the local market, but most of the firm's output is currently exported to China.

Challenges. The firm's main challenges relate to unreliable electricity supply, high electricity tariffs, high fuel prices and an unfavourable tax regime.

Development agenda. The firm intends to continue planting new sisal at the rate of 150 hectares per annum. It also intends to establish clean energy sources to utilize abundant sisal wastes. Plans are under way for the construction of a new factory at Kisangata Estate.

Chapter 11

COTTON

11.1 Sector Profile

Background and overview. Commercial cotton production was introduced into Tanganyika by the German East Africa Company in 1904. Production, based on small-scale farming, expanded under British colonial rule, especially in the Western Cotton Growing Areas (Mwanza, Shinyanga, Mara, Tabora and the Western Lake region). By the 1920s cotton had become an important export crop. By 1951 annual cotton production reached 78,000 bales. Farmers formed primary cooperatives that progressively took control of cotton purchasing. In 1952 the Victoria Federation Cooperative Union and the Tanganyika Lint and Seed Board were established. The primary cooperatives became members of the Victoria Federation Cooperative Union, whose main role was to develop a cotton industry. The main function of the Tanganyika Lint and Seed Board was to market cotton lint from Tanganyika, which had previously been sold through Uganda.

In 1967, as part of the government's centralization of economic activity, the cooperative unions were dissolved. The Tanzania Cotton Authority was formed in 1973 to promote the cotton sector. It took control of production, of the buying of seed cotton from farmers, and of the processing of cotton lint for export. In 1984 the government reinstated the regional cooperative unions under the Tanzania Cotton Marketing Act, which established the Tanzania Cotton Marketing Board. The functions of the Tanzania Cotton Marketing Board were primarily regulatory, but they also included the exporting of cotton lint on behalf of the regional cooperative unions.

In 1993 the government liberalized the industry and formed the Tanzania Cotton Lint and Seed Board as the exclusive regulator. The Cotton Industry Act of 2001 provided for the formation of the Tanzania Cotton Board to promote, facilitate and monitor the production, marketing, processing and export of cotton.

TABLE 11.1. The trend in cotton production 2000–2011.

	WCGA total	(%)	ECGA total	(%)	Seed cotton grand total (mt)	Lint production (mt)	Seed cotton average price (Tanzanian shillings/kg)
2000/01	123,418	99.8	171	0.2	123,589	41,301	180
2001/02	147,575	99.6	567	0.4	148,142	50,885	175
2002/03	187,814	99.6	767	0.4	188,581	62,842	180
2003/04	138,916	99.4	903	0.6	139,819	46,844	280
2004/05	338,402	98.1	3,187	1.9	341,589	114,481	250
2005/06	374,819	99.5	1,772	0.5	376,591	126,228	220
2006/07	129,265	99	1,320	1	130,585	43,771	350
2007/08	199,954	99.9	710	0.1	200,664	67,259	450
2008/09	366,897	99.5	1,544	0.5	368,697	123,546	450
2009/10	266,765	99.1	239	0.9	267,004	89,496	440
2010/11	162,882	99.6	636	0.4	163,518	54,809	800

Source: Tanzania Cotton Board. 'WCGA' stands for Western Cotton Growing Areas. 'ECGA' stands for Eastern Cotton Growing Areas.

Cotton production. Some 400,000 hectares in the Lake Zone are sown with cotton each year by almost half a million smallholder farmers. The cotton crop is wholly rain-fed, and yields an average of 260 kg of lint per hectare.

In the five-year period 2005–9, cotton generated foreign earnings averaging US$92 million per annum. In recent years, almost all cotton production has been in the Western Cotton Growing Areas. The Eastern Cotton Growing Areas currently account for less than 1% of total production but they have potential for increased production. The current low level of production is partly due to higher pest pressure, but also to the availability of alternative economic opportunities in the Eastern region. Table 11.1 shows the trend in cotton production over the last ten seasons.

Profiles and lines of business of large firms. There are about 35 cotton ginneries, all processing cotton lint for the export market. Some ginneries process cotton seed into cotton oil and seed cake.

Lintex (Tanzania) Ltd, established in 1995, procures unprocessed cotton from farmers in 300 villages around the Mara, Mwanza, Shinyanga and Tabora regions. The ginnery is located in Kwimba district in the Mwanza region. The company sells lint cotton to international merchants from Europe, Asia, the Far East and Africa, as well as to local and regional textile mills.

Fresho Ginnery, established in 2000, is situated in the Shinyanga region. The firm buys cotton from farmers in the region and processes it into lint, most of which is sold on the export market. The firm utilizes cotton byproducts such as cotton seeds by milling them into cotton oil and then into cotton seed cake for the manufacture of animal feeds. The company has 100 full-time employees.

S & C Ginning Company Limited was established in 1996 as a subsidiary of the Sumaria Group. The company, located in Bulamba in the Lake Zone, procures unprocessed cotton from farmers and gins it into bales. The company has an oil mill that produces edible oil from cotton seed; it markets this oil domestically. Cotton lint is exported. The company exported cotton lint to the value of $5.4 million in 2010.

Alliance Ginneries is involved in the buying, processing and marketing of cotton. It operates ginneries in Kenya, Tanzania, Zambia and Zimbabwe. The export value of the Tanzanian business in 2010 was US$3.3 million.

Olam (T) Ltd is a subsidiary of Olam international: a leading supply chain manager and processor of agricultural products and food ingredients. The firm has 25 branches in Tanzania and employs 110 full-time staff. In 2010 the firm exported cotton lint worth almost US$14 million, making it Tanzania's largest exporter of cotton lint. The firm also produces cashew nuts, cocoa, pulses and peanuts.

Badugu Ginning Company Limited, which is fully owned by Tanzanians of African descent, is located near Musoma in the Mara region. It employs 500 people and has an annual turnover of around US$3 million.

Birchand Oil Mills Ltd is located in the Nyakato industrial area in Mwanza and has a branch in the Ushirombo district in Shinyanga. It is profiled in the next section.

Lines of business of medium-sized firms. The cotton seed oil produced by ginning companies is usually semi-refined. This leaves an opportunity for medium-sized businesses to refine, pack and brand oil for domestic consumption. Some early entrants of this kind have established well-known brand names.

Small-scale, informal and peripheral activities. Small animal feed producers in Mwanza, Shinyanga and Dar es Salaam use cotton seed byproducts (seed cake) to produce animal feed. There is a growing trade in seed cake. Traders from the Lake Zone sell in Dar es Salaam, Arusha and elsewhere.

Supply and marketing chain. Cotton seeds are grown locally by the Tanzania Coffee Board research centre at Ukiriguru Research Institute in Mwanza and also by a private firm called Quton. Most pesticides are imported and supplied locally: by the Tanzania Coffee Board and by private suppliers operating from ginners' stores.

There are two major channels for cotton trading: the traditional channel is through cooperative societies, which also have ginning facilities; the second is through private traders, who invest heavily in their supply chains. (Most cooperative societies have limited financial capacity compared with private traders.)

Export status and potential. A peak in export earnings occurred in 2005/06, when export revenue reached US$161.1 million. Since then, export earnings have fluctuated with world prices and with the effects of the post-2008 downturn. Export earnings in 2009/10 stood at US$60.4 million. The top five exporting firms (Olam (T), Roshan, S & C Ginning Company, Afrisian and Birchand) accounted for about 64% of cotton lint exports in that year.

Policy context. Cotton yields are low by international standards: 750 kg per hectare, compared with a global average of 2,000 kg per hectare. This is in part a reflection of the lack of adequate extension services.

Over 80% of cotton is exported as lint, so only a limited amount of employment is created in downstream activities. Figure 11.1 shows the industry supply chain.

The government of Tanzania, together with development partners, is taking measures to revive the sector. These measures are aimed at increasing productivity and yields by introducing contract farming, thus revitalizing the textile sector. The Cotton Development Fund supports farmers by giving them access to equipment and by providing loans.

The Tanzania Gatsby Trust works with stakeholders to develop the sector. The programme began in 2008 with two main objectives: to double yields and to stimulate value-adding industries in the textile and clothing sector. The programme's initiatives include the introduction of improved cotton seed, assistance to farmers to help them adopt minimum-tillage/conservation agriculture, and the setting up of contract farming between ginners and farmers. It aims to promote both domestic and foreign investment in the sector. It also funds the Ukiriguru Research Institute for cotton seed production. It has set up plots in various districts to demonstrate alternative production technologies and crop husbandry techniques.

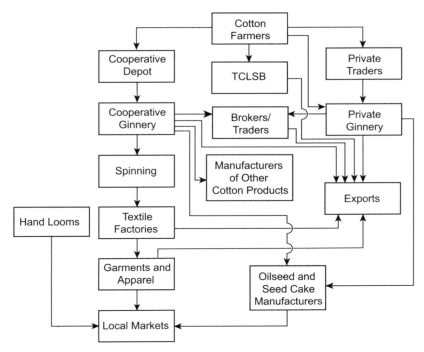

FIGURE 11.1. The cotton supply chain. Source: Tanzania Cotton Board.

Challenges. Apart from the problems noted above (low yields and poor downstream linkages), the industry faces several ongoing problems:

- poor cotton quality;
- low levels of expenditure in research and development activities; and
- poor infrastructure (this relates especially to feeder roads and cotton storage facilities at village level).

The responsibilities of the Tanzania Cotton Board are very broad and it is therefore difficult for it to fulfil its remit given the limited resources available to it. It is required to regulate the industry, inspect the quality of lint, announce indicative prices (a task that has become impractical since 2004), and collect and disseminate statistics. In practice, cotton is seldom inspected at buying posts. In some cases a private company is hired to inspect quality on behalf of the board, but this can lead to corruption.

The cost of utilities is high in Tanzania compared with neighbouring countries.

11.2   Profiles of Major Firms

11.2.1   Badugu Ginning Company Limited (BGCL)

Basic details.   Located in the Mara region, BGCL employs 500 people and has an annual turnover of around US$3 million.

History.   BGCL is one of the few major Tanzanian manufacturing companies that is fully owned by Tanzanians of African descent. The firm is owned by five Tanzanian professionals who started out running a business that bought logs from government forests and made timber for sale. The business later developed into a furniture manufacturing concern. The region in which the firm was located had ample cotton production and the founders saw a new business opportunity in the cotton ginnery field. BGCL formally started its operations in 2006, when it hired some underutilized ginning machines from Nyanza Cooperative Union. In 2007 the company purchased some old machinery that was being disposed of by Mara Oil Mills (a government-owned ginnery) to expand their operation. Until 2009 the manufacturing processes were largely manual, depending on a large workforce of casual labourers. Since 2010, however, most operations have been automated (see below).

Current activities and products.   BGCL is active in ginning and crushing raw cotton. The company works closely with the Tanzania Cotton Board and Techno-Serve (an international NGO) to promote contract farming by educating smallholder farmers about modern practices and to support capacity building for group formation and organization. The company also distributes inputs to contract farmers. There are currently 180 contracted farmers' business groups in the region.

Organization and management.   The five founders act as the board of directors. The chairman of the board acts as managing director and is assisted by professional managers for procurement and logistics, finance, marketing and administration and human resources.

Firm capabilities.   BGCL's current installed daily capacity is 300 cotton lint bales of 200 kg. Its daily crushing capacity is 90 mt.

Supply and marketing chain.   Seed cotton is harvested from farms by members of farmers' business groups. It is weighed by farmers' business group secretaries, witnessed by farmers and stored in well-fumigated stores. The company delivers the cotton to the factory, where it is reweighed, inspected and offloaded to the seed cotton godowns, ready for ginning. After ginning, cotton lint is packed in bales of 200 kg and cotton seeds are dispatched to the oil mill plant for crushing to produce cotton seed oil, cotton seed cake and cotton husks.

Exports.   About 90% of the cotton lint is exported to the UK and the Far East. (Cotton seed oil, cotton cake and husks are sold on the local market.) Customers in the UK include Plexus Cotton Limited, CDI-Cotton Distributors Inc. and Copaco. Customers from the Far East include Saurashtra and Luck Spinning of Thailand.

Recent developments.   In 2009 BGCL took out a loan of US$170,000 to modernize its plant, allowing it to automate most of its production processes. This led to a reduction in its staffing levels of almost 50%.

Development agenda.   The company now plans to set up a soap-making plant, using the waste products from its oil mill.

11.2.2   Olam Tanzania Limited

Basic details.   Olam Tanzania Limited is a subsidiary of Olam International: a supply chain manager and processor of agricultural products and food ingredients. It has 25 branches and employs 110 full-time staff. In 2010 it exported cotton lint worth almost US$14 million, making it the country's largest exporter of cotton lint. The firm also has significant interests in other agricultural products, including cashew nuts, cocoa, pulses and peanuts.

History.   Olam International Limited has a presence in 65 countries and supplies over 11,000 customers. Headquartered in Singapore, Olam International began its operations by exporting cashew nuts from African countries, including Tanzania, to India. It then expanded its business by processing raw cashew nuts into blanched kernels. Over time it expanded into other activities and into other countries. Olam Tanzania was established in 1994.

Current activities and products.   The company sources cotton from farmers, processes it to separate out the seeds, and grades the cotton before packing it into bales. The cotton lint is exported mainly to China, Thailand and the US.

Organization and management.   Olam Tanzania is headed by a zonal business manager who is assisted by zonal managers and field officers. The finance, human resources and field operations departments are run by professional managers.

Firm capabilities. The current installed capacity of Olam Tanzania is 25,000 mt of cotton lint per annum. It operates a contract farming scheme under which farmers are provided with seeds, fertilizer and storage facilities. The company benefits from access to Olam International's resources, including technical personnel, managers, information technology services, and quality-assurance and performance-management systems.

Supply and marketing chain. Cotton collected from farmers is shipped directly to the factory, sorted out to separate the seeds from the lint, graded and packed into bales for export.

Exports. Olam Tanzania accounted for 22% of the industry's export earnings in 2009/10.

Recent developments. The company has extended its operating area to the entire Lake Zone, which includes 16 cotton-growing districts.

Development agenda. The company now plans to establish its own cotton plantations. It also plans to expand its activities into the production of oil from the cotton seeds.

11.2.3 Birchand Oil Mills Ltd

Basic details. Birchand Oil Mills has a total of 100 permanent employees and 300 casual workers. Turnover in 2009/10 was about US$8 million, of which US$6 million came from exports.

History. Birchand Oil Mills was established in 1996 as a subsidiary of the Birchand Group. It began as an oil-processing factory before moving into ginnery activities in 1996. The business uses largely manual processes and employs a relatively large number of casual labourers.

Current activities and products. Birchand Oil Mills collects cotton from various districts of the Lake Zone. The cotton is sorted to separate it from seeds before processing it into cotton cake, cooking oil and cotton bales.

Organization and management. The management team, headed by the CEO and a general manager (in charge of marketing), oversee departments for operations, administration and purchasing.

Firm capabilities. Birchand Oil Mills has a current production capacity of 16–18 cotton bales per hour, which is equivalent to 300,000 bales of cotton per season.

Supply and marketing chain. Cotton is bought from farmers and collected directly by the company's employees, who then deliver it to the factory.

Exports. Cotton bales are exported, while cooking oil and cotton cake are sold via wholesalers on the domestic market. The main export destinations are Kenya, South Africa and India.

Recent developments. Government subsidies of 50% on farmers' production inputs (such as fertilizers, pesticides and equipment) has lowered the costs of production. The factory expects to increase its production to between 600,000 and 1,000,000 bales of cotton per season over the next five years.

Chapter 12

TEXTILES

12.1 Sector Profile

Background and overview. Tanzania's first textile factory, Tanganyika Textiles Ltd, was established in 1959.

Between 1966 and 1985, the textile sector grew rapidly under the aegis of the National Textile Corporation (TEXCO), protected by high import duties and a ban on some imports. In the 1960s and 1970s Tanzania's output fully met domestic demand. By 1985 the total installed capacity was 250 million linear metres of fabric and the industry was one of Tanzania's biggest in terms of employment. Most firms were state owned and fully integrated.

Under the economic reforms of the mid 1990s, most public-sector textile firms were privatized. There are currently 23 established firms, of which 14 are operating. The decline is in large part attributable to the low productivity levels of former parastatals. (However, even after privatization some factories have been closed down due to lack of sufficient raw materials.) The sector employs between 15,000 and 20,000 people, depending on the season. Production capacity has increased from 31 million square metres in 1995 to 150 million square metres in 2008. The trend in production is shown in Table 12.1.

Export sales now stand at US$306.5 million. The trend in exports is shown in Table 12.2.

It is estimated that Tanzania's textile producers consume in the region of 30,0000 mt of cotton lint per annum. Most of the lint is spun into 100% cotton yarns, which are then made into traditional lightweight woven fabrics (khanga and kitenge). A limited amount of Tanzanian cotton is ultimately transformed into regular fabrics that are used locally in the manufacture of apparel.

Tanzania is among Africa's top five producers of conventional (i.e. non-organic) cotton and it is the world's fourth largest producer of organic cotton (after India, Turkey and Syria). However, the supply of cotton lint and yarn to local textile producers is very limited. Most textile producers do

TABLE 12.1. Production of major textile products.

Commodity	2004	2005	2006	2007	2008	2009P
Textile bags (thousands)	1,739	1,837	1,473	2,092	1,590	1,541
Knitted fabrics (thousands of m²)	15,414	11,320	22,832	20,755	14,557	9,554
Knitted garments (thousands)	218	291	400	400	419	404
Cotton yarn (mt)	15,031	11,442	4,677	4,731	5,728	5,791
Woven fabrics (thousands of m²)	115,524	94,881	107,889	109,843	134,717	91,501
Blankets (thousands)	261	284	255	474	269	345

Source: National Bureau of Statistics (2010): Statistical Abstract.

TABLE 12.2. Exports to major markets, 2000–2008 (US$).

Year	Exports to US	Exports to EU
2000	239,612	15,837,824
2001	432,392	20,389,977
2002	328,163	14,372,195
2003	1,927,159	12,575,150
2004	3,352,998	15,393,091
2005	4,099,620	11,828,534
2006	3,717,745	13,042,028
2007	3,281,447	10,865,295
2008	1,872,475	11,922,604

Source: National Bureau of Statistics (2010): Statistical Abstract.

not produce year round due to shortages of raw materials. (Direct exports are more profitable and exporters tend to have forward contracts, leaving insufficient quantities to supply orders from local producers.)

Profiles and lines of business of large firms.

Tanzania–China Textile Friendship Mills was founded in the 1960s as a parastatal but is now a joint venture between the government of Tanzania and a private Chinese company. It employs about 1,200 workers. It is profiled in the next section.

Karibu Textile Mills is a private company, established in 1998, which employs about 900 people. It is profiled in the next section.

21st Century Textiles Limited is a subsidiary of Mohamed Enterprises Tanzania Ltd (METL), which is profiled in Chapter 2. The company employs 300–1,500 people depending on the season, in a factory that formerly belonged to a state-owned textile-processing enterprise, Morogoro Polytex Ltd, which was acquired by METL in 1998.

21st Century Textiles produces cotton and polyester textiles: kitenge fabric, khanga fabric, household linen, Maasi cloth, uniforms, kikhoi and yarn.

21st Century Textiles specializes in customized products. It invites its main clients to develop their own exclusive designs. About half of the firm's business is of this kind, and this has enabled it to maintain production throughot the year, in contrast to most firms in the sector.

Sunflag (T) Limited was established in 1965 and employs more than 2,700 people. It is part of the Sunflag Group, which has offices in Tanzania, the UK, India, Thailand, Nigeria, Kenya and the US. Sunflag (T) is a fully integrated textile and garment company located in Arusha. Its lines of business includes spinning, weaving, knitting, yarn dye, finishing (dying and printing) fabrics, garments, home textiles and mosquito bed nets, and organic and conventional cotton processing. The fabrics that it makes include yarn, dyed kikoi, khanga and kitenge, masai 'shuka' and apparel fabrics. Mosquito nets are made from imported yarns. Its main markets include Tanzania, the EU (mainly the UK), Southern Africa (mainly South Africa), East Africa and the US.

Nida Textile Mills is owned by the Pakistan Cosmos Group and it is related to the Giga Group. Incorporated in Tanzania in 2003, it employs about 1,700 people. Its main lines of business are spinning, weaving, printing and textile make-up. The company spins local cotton to make yarns, which are then made into khanga, kitenge, bed sheets, bed linen, curtains and fabrics. These operations are undertaken jointly with Namera Textile Mills, which is part of the same group. Namera handles spinning and weaving while Nida deals with printing and finishing. Its main export markets are in East Africa, but it also sells to Europe, South Africa and the US.

African Pride Textile Mills is a textile printing company; it employs about 150 people. It prints khanga and kitenge on locally sourced and imported 'greige' fabrics. It has wholly owned wholesale outlets in Uganda, Kenya and Mozambique.

Morogoro Canvas Mills was established in 1983; it employs about 1,300 people. The company produces carded cotton yarn and various types of canvas, filter cloth, tire cord fabrics and material for workwear. It has an in-house processing plant for dyeing and printing. Most of its production involves the spinning and weaving of cotton to make heavyweight canvas products used in the manufacture of tents, tarpaulins and shoes. Its main markets are Southern and East Africa, the US and the Arabian Gulf.

A to Z Textile Mills was established in 1966; it employs about 7,000 people. Its main operations include the production of mosquito nets, knitting fabrics and knitting garments. It extrudes its own yarns and then makes knitted netting that is then cut to make bed nets. The company also knits cotton fabrics and finishes them to make T-shirts and polo shirts. It exports to more than 25 countries, with most of its exports going to Southern Africa and East Africa.

Kilimanjaro Blanket Corporation was established in 1965; it employs about 100 people. It weaves blankets using bought-in yarn and sells almost all its output within Tanzania. It exports a small part of its output to Burundi.

Tanzania Packing Materials (1998) Ltd is part of the Mohamed Enterprises Tanzania Ltd (METL) group of companies. METL owns sisal estates and fibre extraction processing facilities. Tanzania Packing Materials (1998) employs about 600 people in spinning sisal yarns, weaving sisal fabrics and making bags and sacks for the domestic market.

Ellen Knitweave Mills Limited employs about 100 people in making terry towelling, knitted fabrics, knitted garments and nappies for the domestic market. The company also has screen printing and embroidery facilities.

Profile of medium-sized firm.

Ihembe Textiles (2005) Ltd, established in 2005, employs around 30 people in the production of grey fabrics and kikhoi. The company's founder, Edgar Nkunda, had a varied career prior to setting up his present business. The venture began when he approached one of the main suppliers of yarn and convinced him to supply raw materials on credit. He began by making kikhoi, selling the product to wholesalers in Kariakoo. The traders to whom he was selling advised him to imitate Malaysian patterns, which he did, and demand subsequently increased to an extent that he could not cope with. Expansion would have required substantial working capital, to which he had no access at that time.

In 2007 he obtained an order to supply grey fabrics to the African Pride Textiles Co. Ltd, which prints khanga and kitenge products using imported fabrics. To ensure consistency in supply, he asked African Pride Textiles to introduce him to the largest supplier of quality yarn at that time: Tabora Textiles. African Pride Textiles bought all of his output, which amounted to 208,000 metres of grey fabric per annum, but two years later the arrangement ended due to disagreements over price. He then set up his current, similar, arrangement with another local company, Namera Textiles, supplying grey fabric for textiles, batik/tie–dye and other uses.

Other activities. The garments manufacturing sector is relatively small, with seven firms currently operating: Mazava Textiles, Kibotrade, Sunflag, A to Z, Cami Apparel, Ellen Knitweave and African Pride.

There are 32 ginners of cotton, mostly operating during the cotton harvest season (i.e. June–July).

The supply in this sub-sector is dominated by ginners, who sell lint to spinners. There are very few spinning textile producers in Tanzania. Most lint is exported to Asia.

The batik/tie–dye sector is dominated by small firms, selling to the domestic market.

Cotton cultivation employs about 500,000 smallholder farmers, who cultivate an average of 0.2–2.0 hectares per annum. The total area of land under cotton cultivation is estimated to be between 400,000 and 500,000 hectares. However, the average yield of land in Tanzania is low, at approximately 670 kg per hectare, as against 690 kg per hectare in Zambia and Zimbabwe; the average for West Africa is 1,090 kg per hectare.

Cotton farmers sell their produce to either cooperatives or private traders, both of whom sell to ginneries, which in turn sell to spinning mills and textile factories (see Figure 11.1 in the previous chapter).

Policy context. In the 1990s, under economic reforms, price controls on cotton were gradually relaxed. Several firms closed down as they could not compete with low-price imports.

Prior to 1990 marketing was handled by cooperative unions and the Tanzania Cotton Board. This system was abolished by the Cotton Act of 1994, and competition was allowed in both marketing and cotton ginning. This enabled producers to get higher crop prices and to be paid promptly.

The Strategic Trade Policy of 2003 emphasizes the adding of value to locally produced products. The goal of the cotton sector development pro-gramme is to have about 60% of the locally produced cotton lint processed locally, making the nation self-sufficient in textile products, exporting some output and raising total employment in the sector to 36,000 people.

The Gatsby Charitable Foundation and the Tanzania Gatsby Trust are working with stakeholders to improve performance in the cotton and textile sector. Their programme began in 2008 with the objective of doubling yields and encouraging value-adding industries in the sector. Recent interventions include the introduction of improved cotton seed, the provision of assistance to farmers in adopting minimum-tillage/conservation agriculture, and the setting up of contract farming between ginners and farmers. The programme aims to promote both domestic and foreign investment. Gatsby funds the Ukiriguru Research Institute for cotton seed breeding. It has set up a number of demonstration plots in different districts at which various production technologies and crop husbandry techniques are demonstrated. The initiative has also supported the introduction of textile-related courses in key training institutions.

Challenges.   The textile sector faces a number of serious problems.

- Competition from cheap imported end products. The importation of very cheap second-hand clothes, commonly known as mitumba, reduces demand for locally produced clothing. Very cheap clothing imported from Asia also offers intense competition to local producers.
- Global competition for raw materials. Textile companies in Tanzania source their cotton domestically, but this cotton is sold at the world market price; sourcing cotton domestically does not offer a cost advantage.
- Inadequate infrastructure. The railway system is largely inoperative, and roads are often unpaved, making transport costly and problematic.
- Poor quality cotton. Crop husbandry practices are no longer as stringently followed as used to be the case prior to liberalization. Input finance mechanisms and extension services previously supported by the cooperatives and by government were no longer provided after liberalization.
- Regulatory weaknesses. The Tanzania Cotton Board cannot perform all its many functions effectively, given the resources at its disposal. Cotton is seldom inspected at the buying posts. Sometimes, private companies are hired to inspect quality, but this process can lead to corruption.
- The high cost of power.
- Port congestion.
- Poor access to capital.

Exports. The main export markets are the US, South Africa, Europe, Denmark, Mozambique, Malawi, Zambia, the Democratic Republic of the Congo, Burundi, Rwanda, Uganda and Kenya.

Recent developments. In 2009 the Tanzania Cotton Board established the Textile Sector Development Unit, which helps potential buyers of Tanzanian textiles to find local supplies. The Textile Sector Development Unit also helps potential investors by providing information on costs, incentives and market access privileges in export markets.

Some eight companies, including Tanzania–China Textile Friendship Mills, have ceased production because of the scarcity of cotton. (Cotton production in 2010/11 was particularly low.)

Rationale for selecting profiled firms. The profiled firms are among the largest textile producers in the country in terms of employment and sales.

12.2   Profiles of Major Firms

12.2.1   *Tanzania–China Textile Friendship Mills (URAFIKI)*

Basic details. URAFIKI is a vertically integrated company involved in spinning, weaving, printing and textile make-up. The company spins local cotton to make yarns, which are then made into fabrics and a limited range of home textiles. It employs about 1,200 workers.

History. URAFIKI was built by the Chinese in 1968 following a request by the first president of Tanzania, Julius K. Nyerere. It was the first plant built in Tanzania using Chinese aid and was the country's largest textile mill at the time. Since 1996 the company has been owned as a joint venture between the Tanzanian government (49%) and an enterprise from the People's Republic of China (51%).

Current activities and products. The company's two main products are types of cotton fabric: khanga and kitenge. Kanga accounts for around 90% of total production. It also produces a small volume of bed linen and curtains.

Organization and management. The majority shareholder appoints the general manager while the minority shareholder appoints the deputy manager. Key functional units are staffed in the same way: the majority shareholder appoints the manager and the minority shareholder appoints the deputy manager. The company's board of directors has five members, three of whom are Chinese and two of whom are Tanzanian.

Firm capabilities. URAFIKI has sought to remain competitive by focussing on traditional products and designs and has retained the traditional specifications of the products. These specifications cover size, brightness (colour penetration) and thickness as well as the phrases, legends and other forms of words printed onto the material. In contrast to most producers of khanga, URAFIKI is conservative, avoiding wording that might give offence to any particular group. URAFIKI also emphasizes the image of its factory as a symbol of good Tanzanian–Chinese relations. It has maintained a strong customer base, especially among older customers. Public institutions tend to treat URAFIKI as their printer of choice for ceremonial khangas.

Exports. URAFIKI does not presently export.

Recent developments. The company stopped production between August 2011 and June 2012 due to a lack of available cotton.

Development agenda. The company is now planning to diversify ownership by inviting individuals and private companies to invest.

12.2.2   Karibu Textile Mills

Basic details. Karibu Textile Mills was established in 1998. The firm produces traditional African fabrics. The firm is located in the Mbagala area, close to Dar es Salaam. It employs 375 people and had a turnover of US$10 million in 2010.

History. The founder began his career as a trader. From 1993 to 1998 he imported printed fabrics from India, supplying a government-owned textile plant. He realized that if he instead imported grey cloth and set up a printing operation locally, he would already have a steady, large-scale customer in place. The present-day business, while greatly expanded, still continues the founder's original mode of operation. Grey cloth is imported, a four-person design team work with non-proprietary traditional designs, and the production process involves a standard three-stage operation of printing, washing and drying. The operation is relatively labour intensive throughout. A final packaging system involves cutting and packing by hand, both for retail sales (to local markets) and for sales to wholesale buyers. The finished textiles are distributed by the firm's own fleet of small trucks.

Current activities and products. The firm produces a wide range of khanga and kitenge fabrics.

Organization and management. Karibu Textile Mills is a typical family business in that it has a board of directors that consists of family members. The managing director is assisted by an operations manager who is a textiles sector expert from India and is also supported by managers for production, sales, finance and personnel.

Firm capabilities. Karibu Textile Mills has managed to control its production costs and maintain relatively low prices. Tanzania has a limited supply of cotton yarn for domestic textile manufacturers, and most manufacturers do not operate throughout the year. Karibu Textile Mills is one of the very few exceptions to this.

Supply and marketing chain. The firm imports grey fabric from India and South Korea, which is less costly than sourcing it locally. Printing chemicals are imported from China and Pakistan. Other inputs are sourced locally. The firm sells its products in all regions of Tanzania via distribution centres and agents.

Development agenda. The firm is currently constructing a spinning mill as part of a strategy to expand its operations and serve other domestic textile manufacturers with grey fabric, which is in high demand locally.

Chapter 13

HIDES, SKINS AND LEATHER

13.1 Sector Profile

Background and overview. The first tannery in Tanzania, Himo Tanners, was established in 1895. It produced pure vegetable tanned leather for the soles of shoes and sandals. In 1958 Tanganyika Bata Shoe Company Ltd, a subsidiary of Bata Shoe International, began producing footwear in the country.

Between 1967 and 1984 the government established three large-scale tanneries: Tanzania Tanneries (Moshi), built in 1968, was a joint venture between Tanzania and the Swedish government; Morogoro Tanneries was established in 1974 with financial assistance from Bulgaria and came into operation in 1979; and Mwanza Tanneries was built in 1974 with a loan from the World Bank (it began production in 1979). The three factories had a combined annual installed capacity of 2.8 million square metres of leather.

Over this period two state-run shoe companies were in operation. The Bata Shoe Company was acquired through nationalization and renamed Tanzania Shoe Company (Bora). The Morogoro Shoe Company was set up in 1980. The two companies had a combined installed capacity to produce 7 million pairs of shoes per annum.

The leather industry in Tanzania reached its peak level of output during the period 1980–85, with the three government-owned tanneries operating close to full capacity. A period of continuous decline resulted in government divesture of all its tanneries between 1992 and 1995. By the late 1990s most of the tanneries had ceased to operate.

Production rose during the following decade (see Table 13.1). The production of hides and skins has, though, continued to be very erratic in recent years.

The industry is protected by a 40% levy on the export of raw hides and skins, but illegal exports that avoid this levy mean that domestic tanneries cannot acquire the volumes of skins and hides they need in order to operate at full capacity.

TABLE 13.1. The production of hides and skins, 2002/03–2009/10 (pieces).

Year	Hides	Goat skins	Sheep skins	Total
2002/03	1,400,000	800,000	460,000	2,660,000
2003/04	1,600,000	1,200,000	650,000	3,450,000
2004/05	1,600,000	1,500,000	750,160	3,850,000
2005/06	1,660,000	1,400,000	950,000	4,010,000
2006/07	1,980,000	1,520,000	1,200,000	4,700,000
2007/08	2,500,000	1,900,000	1,500,000	5,900,000
2008/09	1,650,000	2,700,000	1,250,000	5,600,000
2009/10	1,500,000	2,400,000	650,000	4,550,000

Source: Ministry of Livestock Development and Fisheries.

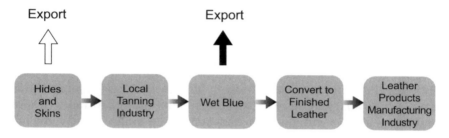

FIGURE 13.1. The leather industry supply chain.

Supply and marketing chain. Raw skins are collected from abattoirs and farms by local collectors, who sell the skins on to large-scale skin traders and tanners. There is a significant deterioration in skin quality both during the collection stage and during tanning, mainly due to poor methods for skinning animals and a lack of proper storage facilities.

Chemicals account for 45% of tanning costs; these are mainly imported from China and Pakistan. Manufacturers sell their products either to wholesale merchants or through their own retail and wholesale outlets (Figure 13.1).

Profiles and lines of business of large firms.

Himo Tanners and Planters Ltd employs 40 permanent employees and had a turnover in 2010 of US$1 million, 90% of which came from exports.

The company, which was founded in 1895 by Mr Sharif Jiwa and his family, was sold in 2002 to Mr Sabas Woisso and Mr Kennedy H. Woisso, who had both been engaged in shoe making and trading since 1994. Prior to their acquisition of the company they had bought finished leather from

Tanzania Tanneries Limited, but when the tanning industry collapsed in the 1990s it became difficult to obtain adequate supplies.

At the time they purchased the factory, it was producing only vegetable tanned leather. Following their acquisition, though, the brothers bought second-hand machines on which they could produce mineral (chrome) tanned leather as well as finished leather for the local market.

The company procures hides and skins from several regions of Tanzania. It mostly purchases wet salted materials: that is, skins that are preserved using salt. The quality of the raw materials is a problem, particularly because of damage caused by hot-iron brand marks on hides and deep knife cuts caused by the use of rudimentary tools during flaying.

The firm exports 90% of its wet blue and 20% of its leather products, mostly to China.

The main products are finished leather (plain and printed upper leather, suede, upholstery leather), which is sold on the domestic market, and vegetable tanned shoulders, which are exported to Kenya. Himo Tanners and Planters also produces footwear, which is sold through the company's own outlets.

JAE Tanzania Ltd, established in 1990, employs 40 people and has an annual turnover of US$185,000.

The company was founded by three partners: Elibariki N. Mmari, a mechanical engineer formerly employed by the Tanzania Electric Supply Organization; Andrew Kassoga, a leather technologist formerly employed at the Tanzania Institute of Leather Technology; and John Rweyunga, a marketing consultant.

The factory was established in response to the collapse of the local leather industry in the late 1980s. The startup was financed by the Small Industries Development Organisation (75%) and the founders (25%). Assistance from the Swedish International Development Cooperation Agency enabled five technical staff to be sent to India for five months of training.

The company's main products are bags, wallets, belts, briefcases, document folders and other small leather items. The company has also established a footwear business and is engaged in the tanning of fish leather.

The company buys its raw hides and skins from the city slaughterhouse and from collectors. Raw fish skins are sourced from fish processing factories.

The company has begun to export a small volume of its output to South Africa, Denmark, China, Kenya and Uganda.

Its medium-term plan is to establish an industrial park for leather firms that will accommodate a modern integrated factory incorporating a tannery and that will undertake the production of footwear, leather goods and leather garments. The company is currently seeking finance through joint venture partners.

Africa Tanneries Ltd (formerly Mwanza Tanneries Ltd) has facilities for processing both hides and skins into wet blue, crust and finished leather. In 1993 Africa Trade Development Ltd took over Africa Tanneries Ltd and spent US$1.5 million on refurbishment, raising production capacity to 1.5 million pieces of chrome tanned leather and vegetable tanned leather per annum by 2004. The tannery is now closed.

Morogoro Tanneries Ltd (formerly Tanzania Leather Industry Ltd), located in Morogoro, was set up in 1974 by the National Development Corporation with assistance from the government of Bulgaria. It began operations in 1978, and the management of the operation was transferred to Tanzania Leather Associated Industries in 1979. It was closed down in 2002 and the assets were sold to Morogoro Tanneries Ltd. The installed capacity is 4,000 pieces of hides and 15,000 sheep and goat skins per day, with a full employment level of between 400 and 500 workers. However, it is operating far below capacity and currently employs only 60 people. Expansion plans have been shelved due to shortage of raw materials (hides and skins).

Ace Leather Tanzania Ltd was established in 2005 as a joint venture between Tanzania Leather Industry Ltd and an Italian partner, Mr Onorato Garavaglia. It is currently the largest tanner in Tanzania, employing about 200 workers. The company produces wet blue cattle hides and goat and sheep skins. The company exports to China, Turkey and Italy.

Afro Leather Ltd was founded in 1987. It closed in 1997 and reopened in April 2003. The company currently produces 200 wet blue hides per day and pickles one or two containers of sheep and goat skins per month.

Kibaha Tannery is part of Industrial Promotion Services, which acquired Tanzania Tanneries (Mwanza).

Moshi Leather Industry employs 40 permanent and 20 casual workers and is currently working at 30% of its capacity. Positioned close to the Kenya border, it has to compete for local raw materials with Kenyan buyers. The tannery needs at least 500 pieces per month of goat and sheep skins to operate at full capacity but currently acquires only about 100 pieces.

TABLE 13.2. Exports of raw hides and skins (2003–9).

Year	Quantity (thousands of kg)	Value (US$)
2003	11,287	6,304
2004	9,385	7,339
2005	6,644	6,335
2006	8,998	7,837
2007	10,569	8,571
2008	5,482	5,107
2009	1,666	1,433
2010	1,789	5,376
2011	2,734	9,268

Source: Tanzania Revenue Authority.

Small-scale, informal and peripheral activities. This sector is dominated by many micro- and small-scale producers engaged in the production of leather products such as shoes, in handicraft production and in local tanning.

Export status and potential. Only around 46% of hides and skins are processed domestically, with the rest being exported (see Table 13.2). There are also some exports of wet blue. All the leather produced by the tanneries is sold on the domestic market apart from a very small quantity that is exported to Kenya.

The major export destinations for Tanzanian skins and hides are Pakistan and China/Hong Kong. Most of the wet blue that is exported goes to Turkey and Italy.

Policy context. There have been a number of interventions in the sector. Between 1989 and 2008 the United Nations Industrial Development Organization supported a leather sector programme for Tanzania. This covers the rehabilitation of slaughter facilities, the provision of equipment to tanneries, the establishment of effluent treatment plants, the supply of basic tools, the provision of technical and entrepreneurship skills for small and medium-scale leather processors, the establishment of common facilities, and the improvement of the policy and regulatory framework. As a result of these efforts the Leather Sector Export Development Strategy (2004), the National Livestock Policy (2006) and the Integrated Leather Sector Development Strategy (2008) were adopted. A levy on the export of raw leather was introduced in 2003, initially at a rate of 20% but this was increased to 40% in 2007.

The main challenge has been in ensuring that an adequate volume of hides and skins is sold to local manufacturers rather than exported. Traders buy raw hides and skins at prices that make local processors uncompetitive, and they export them by smuggling or misdescribing their consignments, thus avoiding the export levy.

Tanning firms complain about the quality of hides and skins: as noted above, these are collected from rural areas via small traders.

Most hides are still being exported in raw form. Nearly all skins (93%) are now processed before export, because the quality of skins has improved substantially (while for hides there has been little improvement). Tanning capacity has been increasing: Moshi Tannery has recently increased its capacity by over 60% and Morogoro Tannery by 100%. New tanneries are being established: SAK International Tannery in Arusha, Salex Tannery also in Arusha, Tanmbuzi Tannery in Moshi and others in Dodoma, Mwanza and Tanga. Four training/production centres have been established. The Institute of Leather Technology in Mwanza has been in operation since 2010. The Tanzania Tanners Association was formed in 2010. Two new associations (the Hide Producers Association and the Leather Products Manufacturers Association) are now also being set up.

Delays in ports and with customs clearance are time consuming. Problems with electricity supply hamper efficiency. Problems with the timely delivery of raw materials to factories, and of exported leather to foreign customers, are commonplace.

Many tanning firms operate using very old equipment, which they acquired second hand.

In the footwear and leather goods industry, the poor quality and availability of domestic leather is a continuing concern. Firms complain of competition from imports of used shoes. A lack of design capabilities and marketing techniques are also cited by firms as serious problems.

13.2   Profiles of Major Firms

13.2.1   Ace Leather Tanzania Limited

Basic details.   Ace Leather Tanzania was established in 2005 as a joint venture between Tanzania Leather Industry Limited and an Italian partner, Mr Onorato Garavaglia. Its factory is located in the Morogoro region.

The company produces semi-processed leather (wet blue cattle hides, goat and sheep skins). Turnover in 2010 was US$4.5 million, 95% of which came from exports. The company currently employs about 200 people.

History. Morogoro Tanneries Limited was established in 1974 by the government of Tanzania through the National Development Corporation and production commenced in 1978. At that time, the tannery had the capacity to produce a little over 900,000 square metres of leather annually. In 1979 ownership of the company was transferred to Tanzania Leather Associated Industries, the government-owned holding corporation for all government-owned businesses in the leather and leather products industry.

The company performed reasonably well in its initial years of operation but by the late 1980s production had declined sharply as a result of adverse economic conditions, which resulted in shortages of the foreign exchange needed for the import of chemicals and machine parts. This resulted in substantial losses.

In the early 1990s the government decided to privatize all state-owned leather and leather products businesses. As a result, Morogoro Tanneries Limited was taken over in 1993 by a private company: Tanzania Leather Industry Limited.

The founders of Tanzania Leather Industry Limited, Mr Rostam Chakaar and Bahram Chakaar, had previously been engaged in the export of raw hides and skins over many years. Their company, Africa Trade Development, was headquartered in Dar es Salaam and had collection centres throughout Tanzania. They saw their acquisition of the tannery as a way to add value to the raw hides and skins that they were dealing in.

At the time of the takeover the tannery had been closed for some time, and the plant and equipment were obsolete. The founders decided to take out a bank loan to upgrade the factory and acquire new, state-of-the-art equipment. By the end of 1997 capacity had been expanded to 1.8 million square metres per annum, making it the largest tannery in Tanzania.

Though this process was completed by 1997, the company did not begin production until later. The new owners had no prior experience in running a leather processing business and it was not until late 2005 that the company entered a joint venture with an Italian partner, Mr Onorato Garavaglia, enabling them to commence production. Mr Garavaglia, a qualified leather technologist, had many years of experience in the leather industry in Italy, Pakistan and elsewhere in Africa.

Current activities and products. The company produces semi-processed leather in the form of wet blue cattle hides, goat skins and sheep skins.

Organization and management. The board of directors consists of the founders and their Italian partner. Day-to-day operations are handled by a managing director, who is assisted by managers for operations, marketing and sales, and finance and administration.

Firm capabilities.   Ace Leather Tanzania is recognized for its use of modern tanning technology. The owners have established connections with major dealers both locally and internationally that ensure a steady supply of raw hides and skins. Mr Garavaglia (the firm's Italian partner) organized the training of key production workers in leather technology.

Supply and marketing chain.   Hides and skins are sourced domestically through a network of agents and collectors. A small proportion of hides and skins come from Zambia, Malawi and Rwanda. Most chemicals are imported, and a minimum of four months' worth of stocks are held in store at all times. Some chemicals—salt, lime, sulphate of ammonia and wattle extract (mimosa)—are available locally.

Exports.   The company exports 95% of its output. China, including Hong Kong, takes over 60% of the total. Higher-quality hides and skins go to Italy and Turkey. Pakistan imports lower-quality wet blue hides and skins.

Challenges.   The major challenges hampering growth and competitiveness are as follows.

- The factory cannot obtain a secure and adequate supply of hides and skins and so operates below capacity. To fill up its capacity, the company allows raw material dealers to use its facilities on a contract basis, thus enabling them to process hides and skins and avoid paying the export levy of 40% of the free on board (FOB) price that they would incur by exporting unprocessed material.

  In collaboration with the Leather Association of Tanzania, the company has been lobbying the government to double the export levy on raw materials and to eventually move towards a total ban on the export of raw hides and skins.

- Power supplies are a major problem. Rationing occurs during dry seasons, and frequent power cuts are caused by deficiencies in infrastructure. Fluctuations in supply often damage machinery and equipment. Electricity shortages have forced the company to install a standby power generator, which is relatively expensive to run.

- Fluctuations in international prices, such as the sharp decline during the downturn of 2008–9, affect the stability of the business.

Recent developments.   The company has upgraded its operations and has moved from a position where it exported only wet blue to a position where over a third of its exports are of crust leather.

Development agenda.   The company plans to double the capacity of the tannery if the supply of raw hides and skins can be assured. This depends heavily on the government's commitment to banning exports of raw hides and skins.

In the medium term the company plans to install a leather finishing plant capable of producing finished leather using the best current technology. It would then be able to supply the manufacturers of leather products with high-quality leather.

Chapter 14

FURNITURE

14.1 Sector Profile

Background and overview. Four companies played a dominant role in the furniture sector from the 1960s to the 1980s. Sikh Saw Mills was established in the 1950s and Kilimanjaro Timber Utilisation Company of Moshi was established in the early 1960s. Both companies were nationalized in 1967. Palray Limited and Afri Metal were established in 1965. These four companies supplied most of the public sector's furniture requirements up to the early 1980s.

In the mid 1980s, following trade liberalization, employment in the furniture industry fell sharply. Palray and Afri Metal expanded their product ranges to include wooden and plastic furniture. Sikh Saw Mills and Kilimanjaro Timber Utilisation were privatized in the early 1990s, by which time their production had fallen to a very low level. Liberalization led to the entry into the sector of a large number of furniture importers. These included Furniture Centre, Japhery Industry Sain Ltd, Furniture and Carpet World, Empress Furniture, Game Store, Quality Centre and Alea Industries. In recent years, the division between local manufacturers and importers has become blurred, as some former importers are now manufacturing locally, while some local manufacturers are importing furniture to complement what they are making in Tanzania. In office furniture, for example, chairs are all made locally. Some companies import medium-density fibreboard (MDF) to make table tops. Some of the large retailers source some of their furniture from locally contracted carpenters.

There are three product categories: contemporary wood and metal household and office furniture; garden furniture made from tropical hardwoods; and general furniture made by hand from tropical hardwoods.

The furniture sector is dominated by a number of local clusters of firms. The most famous is Keko, located near Chang'ombe Road in Dar es Salaam, which began with the establishment of five firms: Matharu Wood Works, Pan African Enterprises, Palray Limited, Jaffery Industry Limited and Kilimanjaro Timber Utilisation. All five were owned by entrepreneurs of Indian origin. There were many individual timber sellers in the same neighbourhood who also made furniture. Over time, many single-person businesses were integrated into small and medium-sized furniture firms and timber sellers, and the cluster developed a reputation for producing quality furniture at reasonable prices.

Mkopi Enterprise Company Limited was established in 2003 in the Keko cluster by two members of the same family. Before starting the company, the founders had been engaged in importing and trading second-hand clothing for more than 15 years. Mkopi Enterprise employs 20 people and had a turnover of US$60,000 in 2010. It exports 60% of its products to Comoro. The firm uses modern cutting machines imported from Japan; it produces sofas, kitchen and dining room sets, beds, office chairs and tables. Mkopi Enterprise uses both domestic and imported hardwoods (the imports come from South Africa). Mkopi Enterprise is now acquiring land for expansion and is setting up a carpentry school. This will expand the range of furniture it produces and will allow the firm to recruit competent skilled labour.

As well as the main clusters of firms, there are many small woodworking units throughout the country that produce doors, windows, beds, cupboards, chairs, tools, tables and shelves. Quality is often low, though, and sales are largely to the local market.

Profiles and lines of business of large firms.   The leading companies in the industry include the following.

New World Furniture Company Limited is profiled in the next section.

Palray Limited is profiled in the next section.

Mandela Furniture Limited is located in the Iringa municipality and manufactures various items of furniture for schools, offices and homes. It has 55 employees and has an annual turnover of about US$500,000.

Mr Felix Aron Mandela, the founder and managing director, learned carpentry from his father and later joined Mawiyo Industries in the Iringa municipality, which made furniture for schools and offices. In 1993, with a capital investment of just US$180, he set up a small workshop using hand tools to make furniture for the home. In 1996 he attended a carpentry course at a vocational education centre to improve his skills, and thereafter the business grew substantially as he secured orders from institutional customers. He recruited graduates from the same vocational training centre that he himself had attended, installed electric tools and bought trucks for procurement of timber and delivery of orders. In 2003 the business was relocated to a Small Industries Development Organisation industrial estate, where there were facilities for expanding the operation.

The firm sources hardwood from suppliers from Tunduru Songea and softwood from within the Iringa region. Some accessories are bought from local hardware shops; about a third of accessories are imported from China. The company has a fleet of four vehicles for undertaking direct delivery to customers.

In 2010 the firm took out a bank loan of US$75,000 to buy additional modern machinery, and it now plans to buy a dry kiln and generator for processing its own raw timber.

Holtan Furniture Industries began in 1996 as a company that fitted out shops. Later it expanded into a joinery factory specializing in interior work for the hospitality, commercial and residential sectors. It began producing solid wood flooring in 1998. The company has its own sawmills at Mangula, in central Tanzania, close to its sources of raw materials. Modern kilns dry the timber to international standards.

Mingoyo Sawmill Company Ltd is a division of the Mingoyo Group, which also includes Maridadi Timberworks. The group's interests extend to Zanzibar and Mozambique. Mingoyo Sawmill was acquired in 1996 from the Tanzania Wood Industry Corporation, which was established in 1980 as a parastatal to manage all wood-based public companies. Mingoyo Sawmill Company Ltd manufactures semifinished components for musical instruments (clarinets, bagpipes and oboes) for export. Mingoyo Sawmill supplies almost 80% of the inputs of Maridadi Timberworks, which manufactures furniture, doors and frames.

Supply and marketing chain.   Tanzania has an abundance of high-value tropical hardwood forests. Timber is shipped to furniture makers, who are mostly located close to urban areas. Most timber suppliers have developed long-term relationships with furniture companies.

Challenges.   The main challenges facing the sector are as follows.

- Hardwood timber stocks are dwindling and remaining supplies are expensive.
- Semi-finished furniture products (components) attract the same duties as finished products, making it hard for local manufacturers to compete with imports.
- There is substantial corruption in the public sector tendering process.

- The cost of borrowing is extremely high (18% or more).
- The high cost and unreliable supply of power hampers local manufacturers relative to importers.

Policy context.   There is no clear public procurement policy aimed at
supporting domestic furniture makers. In 2011 the government announced
that it would only buy furniture made locally from hardwood. However, the
supply of hardwood timber is limited, and one could reasonably argue that
the best policy would be to discourage further felling of the remaining trees
in the natural forests. With changing technology, high-quality and durable
furniture is being made locally using softwood and imported components
such as MDF. It has been argued that it would be better for government to
buy domestically made furniture regardless of the raw materials used.

14.2   Profiles of Major Firms

14.2.1   *New World Furniture Company Limited (NWFCL)*

Basic details.   NWFCL is a subsidiary of the New Age Construction Company Limited (NACC), which is located in Arusha. NACC has 110 employees,
60 of which are employed within NWFCL. NACC has an average annual
turnover of about US$1.5 million.

History.   NACC's founder, Mr Godson Ngomuo, began working in the
construction industry in Nairobi (Kenya) after completing primary edu-
cation in 1983. He was initially employed by various companies engaged
in construction and in the wood sector, in positions varying from casual
labourer to foreman. In 2004 Mr Ngomuo decided to move to Arusha in
Tanzania and there, together with his wife, he founded NACC. Initially, the
company was mainly engaged in the construction of residential buildings.
NWFCL was established in 2007 as part of a strategy for expansion into the
furniture sector. The startup was financed by the owners' own funds and
loans acquired from friends and relatives. The company began with seven
employees and attained an initial annual turnover of about US$80,000.

Current activities and products.   NACC is now mainly involved in residential construction and with the manufacture of building materials,
including bricks and floor tiles. NWFCL is involved in designing, manufacturing, repairing and supplying various items of furniture for domestic,
commercial and public sector buyers. It employs 60 people and has an
average annual turnover of about US$1 million. Its main products include

hardwood office tables, conference tables, office chairs, bookshelves and cabinets, dining tables and chairs, kitchen cabinets, partitions, doors, windows, sofas and flooring.

Organization and management.   Mr Godson Ngomuo serves as the managing director of NACC, whose corporate office manages NWFCL. The technical director of NWFCL manages the company in Mr Ngomuo's absence. NWFCL has four departments: administration, technical, marketing and sales, and accounting.

Firm capabilities.   The firm has a well-established customer network of government and private institutions, including banks, hotels, hospitals, colleges and schools. Its workshop is well equipped, and by installing modern woodworking machinery it has steadily improved productivity and quality. NWFCL benefits from the experience and support of NACC's board, which oversees all aspects of the business.

Supply and marketing chain.   The company gets its major inputs from local agents, with a few inputs imported from Kenya. Key customers contact the company directly. The company delivers to the customers' premises within the Arusha urban area.

Challenges.   The company faces strong competition from imported furniture, especially from China. The costs of production in Tanzania are very high compared with neighbouring countries. The level of taxes, electricity costs and problems with the reliability of power supply are serious challenges. Problems with the supply of timber can lead to periodic suspensions in production. Nonetheless, in contrast to most firms in the industry, NWFCL has managed to remain viable by delivering high-quality products and services at competitive prices.

Recent developments.   NWFCL was recently appointed by Vodacom to renovate its shops across ten regions of the country. This has substantially improved the image and visibility of the firm among potential commercial clients.

Development agenda.   The firm is keen to find a suitable investor who can inject capital and invest in plant and equipment so that it can expand its operations. The company does not currently export, but it has plans to export to neighbouring countries in East and Central Africa in the near future.

14.2.2   Palray Limited

Basic details.   Palray, which was one of Tanzania's first furniture firms, pioneered a number of products in the country in the 1960s, including fabricated window and door grills and tricycles for the disabled. The company, which operates from Dar es Salaam, employs about 65 full-time and 35 casual employees. Its annual turnover is about US$1.2 million.

History.   Palray was established in 1965 by Mohinder Singh. Prior to founding Palray, Mr Singh worked as a technician with a private company whose Greek owner specialized in metal fabrication. In 1965 he set up a small business dealing with the fabrication of kindergarten play furniture. His product range later expanded to include window and door grills, tricycles for the disabled and hospital and school furniture. Between 1965 and the mid 1980s, Palray expanded substantially: at one time the company employed 200 people. During this period Palray developed into a holding company, under the umbrella of which were companies producing melamine crockery, plastics, steel wool, iron beds and springs. Its furniture activities were carried out by a company named East African Furniture; it was the major supplier of furniture and related products to governmental and non-governmental institutions in Tanzania during this period. Following liberalization of the economy from the mid 1980s, most of Palray's subsidiaries could not withstand competition from imports and the depreciation of the Tanzanian shilling and they were either sold off or closed down. The furniture operation was reintegrated into Palray Limited. Over 100 employees lost their jobs in the process.

Current activities and products.   Palray's traditional business has been the manufacture of furniture from locally sourced and imported raw materials. Current products include office furniture, school furniture, hospital furniture and laboratory equipment. The products are made from a range of materials, including hardwood, softwood, MDF, plastic and steel. The main market for its products is the government and its agencies, which account for about 70% of sales.

Organization and management.   The company operates under a managing director, who reports to the board of directors. Under the managing director are a general manager and a financial controller. These positions are held by well-trained and experienced professionals.

Firm capabilities.   Palray is known in the market for its wide range of quality products and reliable service, and it has won various awards over the years. It is one of the few furniture makers in the country with machinery for undertaking sandblasting, which cleans metal products to completely remove oil and dust.

Supply and marketing chain.   About 50% of the company's raw materials are sourced locally. The main imports are MDF, consumables and pipes. Imports are primarily sourced from China and Malaysia. Palray has an outsourcing arrangement with a company based in Dubai that takes care of its import requirements.

Recent developments.   The company has increased its use of MDF in furniture making in response to changing technology, an increasing preference for gloss-finished furniture, a shortage of wood and increased competition.

Development agenda.   Palray plans to introduce powder-coating plants, stainless steel cutting machines and welding machines to enhance the quality of its product and its overall competitiveness.

Chapter 15

CONSTRUCTION

15.1 Sector Profile

Background and overview. When Tanganyika became independent in 1961, the country had only two local architects, six engineers and no private contractors. Most construction work was executed by the Public Works Department, while some large projects were undertaken by contractors from Kenya and Israel, which were also the source of most imported building materials.

After independence, construction projects, which were often donor-funded, attracted foreign contractors and architectural and engineering firms. A number of local contractors were established, mainly owned by former building foremen of Asian origin. Following nationalization under the Arusha Declaration of 1967, foreign investment in the industry declined. The state-owned Mwananchi Engineering and Construction Company was established to undertake construction activities. This period saw the emergence of many small, local building contractors, with varying levels of competence.

The local distribution of building materials was carried out by a monopoly, and access to foreign currency was restricted. As a result, firms' access to raw materials was restricted. Newly established state-owned cement, steel and aluminium firms suffered from managerial problems, resulting in erratic and inadequate supply. A lack of competent staff led to serious quality deterioration, while corruption was a continuing problem.

The construction industry experienced further turbulence in the period following the Idi Amin War in 1978, when foreign currency restrictions became even more stringent. Many projects had to be suspended due to lack of funds, and some foreign contractors left the country. Local contractors improvised with locally available materials, using terrazzo for bathtubs and washbasins in housing projects, for example.

During this period construction-related courses were introduced at the University of Dar es Salaam, Ardhi College, Dar es Salaam Technical College, Ifunda and elsewhere.

From the mid 1980s economic reforms improved the availability of construction materials and access to new technology. The closure of many parastatals resulted in the construction industry's temporary decline, and to the re-emergence of private-sector developers. The Integrated Roads Project, which began with donor funding in the early 1990s, recommended that government should withdraw from direct involvement in implementing projects. The project helped to develop local private civil works contracting, and consulting capacity. Demand could not be met by local contractors and consultants, and this led to an influx of foreign civil contractors and consultants. The Integrated Roads Project was also associated with the establishment of the (now-defunct) Plant & Equipment Hire Company in 1991, which provided local contractors with access to equipment.

The contribution of construction activity to GDP has grown from 6.1% in 2004/05 to 6.8% in 2009/10. The industry comprises a number of major segments.

Transportation and communication: roads and public works, bridges, airports, sea ports, telecommunication systems and related physical infrastructure.

Water works and sanitation projects: water supply, sanitation and sewage schemes, dams, irrigation systems and related physical infrastructure.

Energy: power stations, power transmission lines, schemes for producing renewable energy, and related physical infrastructure.

Buildings: residential buildings and estates, slum redevelopment, hospitals, schools and other educational facilities, hotels, touristic facilities, factories, shops, commercial and industrial buildings and related physical infrastructure.

Other physical infrastructure: defence, mining, agriculture and related areas.

Infrastructure development by the government constitutes the largest sector of the construction industry. This has focused on roads, irrigation, dams and water supply, energy projects and public building projects (schools, hospitals and academic institutions). Public housing projects have been in decline; here, the private sector and pension funds have become the primary investors.

Policy context. The Construction Industry Development Strategy of 1991 and the Construction Industry Policy of 2001 were enacted to promote the development of the industry. The legislation was augmented by the establishment of three regulatory bodies in 1997: the Contractors Registration

Board, the Architects and Quantity Surveyors Registration Board and the Engineers Registration Board. The Public Procurement Act of 2001 led to the establishment of the Public Procurement Regulatory Agency and the Public Procurement Appeals Board. The Public Procurement Act of 2004 and the presence of the Public Procurement Regulatory Agency have contributed to openness, transparency and efficiency in public works procurement. Calls for further reforms led to the Public Procurement Act of 2010.

A decision to finance development through the use of locally generated funds has accelerated infrastructure development: an area that previously depended mainly on donors. A two-and-a-half-fold increase in funds for road building in 2007/08 led to some initial problems in absorbing available finance. The National Housing Corporation is now being reformed to focus on development, as opposed to simply managing existing properties. The Tanzania Building Agency has been established to develop and maintain government buildings. Pension funds, which have traditionally invested in commercial accommodation schemes, are now beginning to invest in low-cost housing for urban areas.

In 2010 a requirement for foreign consultants to partner with local consultants in the fields of architecture, engineering and quantity surveying was introduced by the Association of Consulting Engineers Tanzania and the Architects and Quantity Surveyors Registration Board. This requirement does not apply to contractors. The absence of a building code has been blamed in some quarters for poor building design, construction and supervision.

Local contractors were responsible for only around 10% of projects by value in 1999. This proportion has increased rapidly, however, and reached 40% in 2010. The Public Procurement Act of 2004 provides for preferences in favour of local contractors on projects valued below US$667,000. However, the provisions of the Act are not strictly enforced, and foreign contractors are sometimes used on projects whose value is far below the official threshold.

Some private developers have failed to employ appropriate consultants, and this has been blamed for a number of serious failures, including the collapse of buildings.

The main players in the industry are as follows.

Government and public institutions. The Ministry of Works is responsible for policy, for the core trunk, regional and district road network, for public buildings, for aerodromes and for overseeing the construction industry. The Roads Fund Board raises funds for the maintenance and upkeep of roads. The Tanzania Roads Agency maintains the national road network (trunk roads and regional roads): a total of 33,012 km. The 'district and feeder roads', a total of 56,018 km, are mainly the responsibility of local government.

Contractors. The 6,309 contractors on the register of the Contractors Registration Board are categorized into five groups: building, civil, electrical, mechanical and specialist. All but the specialist contractors are classified into seven grades, with Class I being the highest grade and Class VII the lowest. Specialist contractors are divided into three classes, with I being the highest and III the lowest.

Some 97% of the firms are Tanzanian. Foreign firms are allowed to register only in Class I. Of the 6,309 contractors, only 7% are deemed to be capable of executing contracts valued above US$2 million. Of these large-scale firms, 56% are local and 44% foreign. Local firms include Afriq Engineering & Construction Co. Ltd, Estim Construction Company Ltd, Southern Link, Namis Corporate and Shibat Enterprises Ltd. Foreign firms include China Railway Jianchang Engineering Co. Ltd, Noremco Construction and Konoike Construction Company Ltd.

About 20% of registered contractors are classed as medium scale (Class II specialists or Class III–V otherwise), capable of executing contracts valued at US$200,000–2,000,000. These include Fabec Investment Ltd, Kiure Engineering and Del Monte (T) Ltd.

The Contractors Registration Board analysed 3,589 projects that were registered with it in 2010, the total turnover of which was US$1.9 billion. Of these projects, 76.4% by value were undertaken by large contractors, 51% of whom were foreign. Medium-sized and small firms executed 19.1% and 4.5% of the works, respectively, by value.

Architects, quantity surveyors, engineering professionals and consulting firms. As of 2010, the Architects and Quantity Surveyors Registration Board had 171 architectural firms and 172 quantity surveying firms on its lists. (About 8% of both groups are foreign.) It also listed 318 architects, 188 quantity surveyors and 126 architectural and quantity surveying technicians and draftsmen. The leading firms include Land Plan Icon, MD Consultancy and Sumar Varma Associates.

As of 2010, there were 3,784 professional engineers (16.5% of whom were foreign), 307 engineering consulting firms (22.5% foreign) and 5,994 graduate and technician engineers on the register of the Engineers Registration Board. Leading engineering consulting firms include TANConsult and Inter-Consult. The latter is a multidisciplinary firm that also undertakes architectural, quantity surveying and project management activities.

The Association of Consulting Engineers Tanzania successfully advocated a law that makes it mandatory for foreign architectural and quantity surveying firms to partner with local firms in the execution of projects. This, together with capacity building programmes instigated by the Association of Consulting Engineers Tanzania, has led to the development of the local consulting industry. Strategic alliances and partnerships have allowed a number of local contractors and consultants to become major players, both locally and regionally.

Associations. The Architects Association of Tanzania, the Tanzania Institute of Quantity Surveyors and the Association of Consulting Engineers Tanzania are all well established. The Contractors Association of Tanzania represents contractors' interests. The Tanzania Civil Engineering Contractors Association represents the interests of contractors involved in civil works.

Competition.   Contracting is dominated by foreign firms. While only 3% of contractors are foreign, they execute 60% of all works by value. Chinese contractors, who entered the scene only 15 years ago, dominate the market. They now constitute 26% of all foreign contractors in terms of numbers. Other firms come from South Africa (21% of all foreign firms), Kenya (11%), Italy (4.6%) and France (2.8%). Chinese contractors are usually backed by Chinese financial institutions and suppliers. Non-Chinese contractors have sometimes employed Chinese foremen to inculcate Chinese culture and methods into their operations. Some Chinese employees in Chinese construction firms have partnered with locals to establish firms with majority local ownership, which allows them to gain preferential treatment in tendering.

Supply and marketing chain.   Cement, aggregates and some steel are produced locally. Steel imports have been rising because of supply and quality problems with locally produced steel. The main sources for imported steel are China, Turkey and South Africa. Glazing, paint, PVC, concrete, aluminium and timber products are increasingly being produced domestically by companies such as Kiboko Paints Ltd, Palray Ltd, ALAF Ltd and Southern Link Ltd. Challenges in ensuring the quality of timber and concrete products as well as the reliability of their supply have led some major contractors to establish their own quarry operations, concrete products workshops and timber workshops. Bitumen, a crucial element for tarmac roads, is wholly imported. Credit arrangements with domestic and international suppliers are crucial for the large construction companies, and lack of access to credit is a serious problem for smaller firms.

Challenges.   The industry faces a number of challenges.

Corruption. Transparency International estimates that about 10% of the money spent on construction activities in Tanzania, amounting to US$28.6 million per annum, is lost to corruption. Some foreign contractors, who were a source of technology transfer to the industry, have left, citing corruption as a factor influencing their decision. Current initiatives aimed at combating corruption include the Construction Sector Transparency Initiative and the Project Anti-Corruption System. The Project Anti-Corruption System is an initiative of the not-for-profit Global Infrastructure Anti-Corruption Centre, which provides guidelines, frameworks and resources to assist in the detection and prevention of corruption on construction projects.

Limited access to construction equipment. Plant and equipment is widely available both for sale and for hire. However, the lack of favourable financing mechanisms constitutes a serious barrier for small contractors. Efforts made by the Contractors Registration Board to ease the problem have resulted in value added tax and import taxes being waived on the purchase of generic construction equipment. Recent initiatives under the Tanzania Lease Finance Act may help to ease the problem further in the future.

A shortage of technical skills. Essential specialized skills are scarce, resulting in high costs. Appropriate skills are not developed within firms, nor are they provided in commercial training schools or technical schools.

A lack of access to finance. There are concerns about firms' access to finance. Requirements such as 100% collateral on bid bonds and performance bonds are seen to be stringent; in most other countries the collateral and performance bond requirements are lower. The Tanzania Lease Finance Act has been enacted but its regulations have not yet come into force. When they do, they will provide a regulatory framework that allows financial institutions to commit larger sums to leasing.

Shortcomings in management. Most domestic construction companies began as small family-owned businesses, and the owners have been reluctant to relinquish control. Many lack governance structures that ensure accountability of the owners to stakeholders. Local contractors are often weak when it comes to planning and often hire incompetent personnel. Funds are often mismanaged and misallocated, record keeping is inadequate and financial control is poor.

Payment problems. Non-payment and late payment both occur in both government and private-sector contracts. The government recently admitted that contractors and consultants, both local and foreign, are owed a total of US$300 million in outstanding payments on public contracts.

Execution of contracts. There is a problem, particularly in local government, with writing and enforcing appropriate contracts due to a lack of managerial capacity. Contract enforcement is expensive and slow. On the other hand, small contractors perceive that many public contracts, which are modeled on the World Bank Contract for Small Works, operate to their disadvantage.

Price fluctuations in construction materials. There is a high degree of volatility in the prices of inputs, while many of the public contracts are fixed, in terms of price, and this can be problematic for contractors.

A weak supply base. Because many downstream actors are small, contractors undertaking large projects face difficulties in sourcing sufficient quantities of inputs. They are forced either to establish their own supply through backward integration, or to import their requirements, or to develop the capacities of their suppliers.

Lines of business of major and medium-sized firms.

China Railway Jianchang Engineering Co. Ltd is a well-established, large-scale Chinese firm. It has the ability to undertake and deliver large and complex projects. It is profiled in the next section.

Konoike Construction Company Ltd is a Japanese construction firm that has established an innovative mentoring approach for local companies, which it now subcontracts to execute most of its works.

Southern Link Ltd is a local construction firm with a strong performance record and a well-defined corporate governance structure, which is uncommon among local contractors.

Afriq Engineering & Construction Co. Ltd, established in 1995 as a partnership between two graduates, has managed to survive successive challenges and has grown to become a Class I contractor.

Noremco Construction, a Norwegian company, is one of the few long-established foreign firms that have survived the arrival of Chinese contractors over the past decade.

Namis Corporate is an electrical and specialist construction firm handling high-voltage projects. It was established by a young former staff member of the Tanzania National Electricity Company who was seeking an opportunity in the private sector. He has built up a substantial business in electrical works.

Inter-Consult Ltd is one of the country's few well-established multidisciplinary firms, combining architectural, engineering, quantity surveying and project management services.

Land Plan Icon is an architectural firm that has effectively executed a number of landmark iconic projects.

Profiles of selected medium-sized firms.

Estim Construction Company Ltd began as a Class VII construction company and is currently registered as a Class I building, civil and mechanical contractor. It has a turnover of around US$75 million.

Estim was established in 1993 by Mr Girhibhai Pindoria, a civil engineer. Estim initially operated as a supplier of manpower, operating as a subcontractor to M/S Konoike Construction Company Ltd, a Japanese civil works contractor. (The owner had worked for Konoike for four years as a site engineer until 1993, when he left to establish Estim.) Konoike provided the founder with an office in its premises, and within a few months Estim began taking on small construction contracts, initially from Konoike and later from others, eventually establishing itself as a major contractor in its own right.

Afriq Engineering & Construction Co. Ltd is a limited-liability Class I building and civil works contractor. It was established by two graduate entrepreneurs, Thadeus Koyanga and Charles Bilinga. The firm employs around 40 people and has an annual turnover in the region of US$12 million.

In 1995 the two directors together with thirteen other new engineering graduates teamed up after they graduated and formed five companies, one of which was Afriq Engineering & Construction Co. Ltd. They brought these companies into a joint venture allied to the National Construction Council (a construction industry advisory body) and the (then named) National Income Generation Programme (a poverty-reduction programme funded by the United Nations Development Programme). The concept involved the National Construction Council giving the joint venture company six months of training on construction management, the National Income Generation Programme nurturing it by meeting startup costs, and the (then-named) Plant & Equipment Hiring Co. Ltd. leasing them heavy equipment. The startup costs were to be refunded as the joint venture began to generate revenue. This original venture failed, however, when the National Income Generation Programme withdrew its involvement. Koyanga and Bilinga then began a new, smaller-scale venture, operating as Afriq Engineering & Construction Co. Ltd.

Initially established in 1995 as a Class VII contractor, Afriq Engineering & Construction has gradually grown to become a Class I building contractor and a Class III civil works contractor.

Kiure Engineering Ltd is a young and fast-growing company based in Arusha that is aiming to move beyond its current registration status as a Class VI building, civil and mechanical contractor. The firm has a workforce of 25 employees and an annual turnover of around US$1 million: a threshold not typically achieved by construction firms of this size.

The firm was established in 2004 as a small construction support unit, providing construction materials to contractors. Upon graduating in engineering in 2000, Omar Kiure established a small mining operation, which he subsequently closed down, prior to establishing Kiure Engineering in 2004 with two other shareholders.

The company is involved in building, civil and mechanical works. Its main operations are the construction of houses, roads, bridges, walls and fences, sign boards, advertising billboards and communication towers and the manufacture of remote-controlled gates ('smart gates') and a variety of other metalwork. It is also involved in the supply of building materials and hardware.

15.2   Profiles of Major Firms

15.2.1   China Railway Jianchang Engineering Co. Ltd (CRJE)

Basic details.   CRJE is a Chinese-owned company that was incorporated in Tanzania in 2000. The company is registered as a Class I building and specialist mechanical contractor. It has 472 employees and its turnover was over US$102 million in 2010.

History.   CRJE was formed in 2000 from a construction unit that had been involved in the construction and maintenance of the Tanzania–Zambia railway line, which was financed by the Chinese government. The company, which is headquartered in Dar es Salaam, has expanded its operations over the past decade via branches in Zanzibar, Dodoma, Arusha and Mwanza.

Current activities and projects. The company is primarily involved in building projects. It has built its reputation through a number of land-mark projects: the ongoing 30-storey Millennium Towers Phase II project; the Uhuru Heights complex; the NSSF Waterfront; ILO–Kazi House; and Mpingo House. Through its subsidiary, CRJE Estates, it is now becoming active in real estate. In partnership with the Mwalimu Nyerere Foundation, it has recently acquired a loan of US$10 million from the International Finance Corporation for the development of the proposed 20-storey Mwalimu Nyerere Towers in Dar es Salaam's city centre.

Organization and management. China Railway Construction Engineering Group Co. (Tanzania) Ltd and Shenzhen Investment Co. (Tanzania) Ltd are the main shareholders. The managing director, a professional civil engineer, reports to a board of directors and oversees operations through six divisional heads.

Firm capabilities. CRJE has built a reputation, with both public- and private-sector clients, for timely delivery and quality work. The company can handle several complex projects in different parts of the country simultaneously. It also provides design services. The firm is ISO 9001 certified and ISO 14001 Environmental and OHSA 18001 Health compliant. CRJE was recognized as the best foreign contractor by the Contractors Registration Board of Tanzania in 2009.

Supply and marketing chain. CRJE has a well-equipped workshop that supplies furniture, timber products and related inputs. CRJE has good working relations with Chinese financial institutions, giving it easy access to guarantees and bonds.

Recent developments. CRJE is now aiming to establish itself in road construction and other civil works. The company is also exploring markets in neighbouring countries.

15.2.2 Konoike Construction Company Ltd

Basic details. Konoike Construction Company is an international construction company based in Japan that has eight branches in Asia and Africa, including one in Tanzania. The company has about 1,700 Japanese staff and a global turnover of just under US$2.3 billion. The Tanzanian branch has about 100 employees (including both expatriate and local employees) and an annual turnover of about US$8 million.

History.   The company was established in 1871 by Mr Chujiro Konoike in Osaka, Japan as a private firm specializing in construction and transportation. The company expanded its operations to Northern Kyushu in 1908 and to Tokyo and Hokkaido in 1915. In 1918 the firm was incorporated as a joint-stock company.

Konoike Construction Company first entered Tanzania in 1979. It is registered as a Class I building and civil works contractor.

Current activities and projects.   Konoike focuses on large projects funded by the Japanese government or Japanese corporations. It concentrates on project management and leaves most operations to local subcontractors. This mode of operation gives it access to local networks and knowledge, allows it to operate with a relatively modest stock of equipment, and avoids the problems of managing a large local workforce.

Konoike has been involved in the construction of roads, bridges, irrigation schemes, schools and markets. It has recently been awarded a US$58.7 million project for the widening of the Mwenge–Tegeta section of the New Bagamoyo Road in Dar es Salaam.

Organization and management.   At its headquarters in Japan, Konoike Construction Company has a board comprising both executive and non-executive directors. The activities of its subsidiaries and branches worldwide are monitored from the company's headquarters.

Firm capabilities.   The firm has facilitated capacity building in a number of local firms, through subcontracting and mentoring arrangements, which has led to these firms growing to become large local contractors. These include Ravji Construction Co. Ltd, Estim Construction Company Ltd, Mac Contractors, Kibafu Construction Co. Ltd and Highland Estates Co. Ltd.

Konoike was awarded the Best Contractor Supporting the Construction Industry award by the Contractors Registration Board in 2006.

Supply and marketing chain.   The firm supplies its own ready-mixed concrete, precast concrete products and aggregates from its own quarry. It also has a well-established asphalt plant for road works.

15.2.3   Fabec Investment Ltd

Basic details.   Fabec Investment deals mainly with civil works and telecommunications infrastructure; it has regional offices in Kenya, Egypt, Zimbabwe, Congo, the Democratic Republic of the Congo and Uganda. Fabec Investment is registered as a building, civil and telecommunication specialist contractor; it employs more than 200 regular employees as well as some 500 individuals on short-period contracts. Its annual turnover is around US$3 million.

History.   Fabec Investment was established in 2003 by Joel Makyao, an engineer, and his wife Mary, an information technology expert. After graduating with a civil engineering degree in 1997, Mr Makyao worked on an informal basis as an architect for individual home builders, while also operating a hardware retail store in Mwanza with his brother. He then took a job with Tritel, a local mobile phone company (which was bought by, in turn, Celtel, Zain and then Airtel), taking responsibility for supervising contractors involved in the construction of telephone towers, initially in Tanzania and then in Uganda in collaboration with his brother.

In 2004 he took a year's unpaid leave from his job in Uganda to return home, and during that year he took a short-term contract at Plessey, Celtel's main supplier, to supervise an installation project in Dar es Salaam. To fund this subcontracting job he needed to take on staff; to do this he borrowed money from a moneylender at 20% interest per month. The job was a success, and in 2005 he began regularly hiring employees as a flow of new contracts came in, not only from Celtel and Plesssey but also from Ericsson, Huawei and other international contractors.

Current activities and projects.   Besides its core business in construction and telecommunication infrastructure, Fabec Investment has ventured into plant and equipment hire, mining exploration, tour and car hire, logistics, metalwork production and warehouse provision. Fabec Investment currently has contracts worth US$8.5 million on hand.

Organization and management.   Joel Makyao is chair and CEO, while his wife Mary is director of finance. The firm has a board of directors constituting both executive and non-executive members, which is broadly representative of the countries in which Fabec Investment operates. Day-to-day operations are run by a general manager.

Firm capabilities.   Fabec Investment executes both publicly and privately financed works both in Tanzania and across the region. Its main source of revenue is the telecommunications sector, but its building and construction activities are expanding. Notable projects executed by the firm include a fibre-optic project in Harare, Zimbabwe, and a network installation in Uganda. Fabec Investment has used a series of strategic partnerships to facilitate its expansion. Each country division is semiautonomous, with all country managers being members of the executive management and the board. Some 45% of Fabec Investment's business is now outside Tanzania, with the Democratic Republic of the Congo and Uganda accounting for over two-thirds of all foreign business.

Supply and marketing chain.   The company periodically supplies aggregates, bricks and other construction inputs to its projects.

Recent developments.   Fabec Investment aims to become the leading service provider for telecommunication and civil works in Africa. The company aims to implement a gradual expansion programme to extend its activities into Malawi, Zambia, Angola, South Africa, Sudan, Nigeria and Mozambique. It is currently taking on projects in road works so as to better position itself in the construction sector. Fabec Investment also plans to build a real estate business.

   The firm has recently formed a mineral consultancy and exploration firm, under the auspices of which it is acquiring mining licenses.

Chapter 16

CEMENT AND BUILDING MATERIALS

16.1   Sector Profile

Background and overview.   Building materials is a broad sector, encompassing cement, paints, timber, aggregates, precast products and tiles. Steel, plastic and glass are dealt with in other chapters.

Cement manufacturing.   Two types of cement are produced in Tanzania: pozzolana and Portland limestone cement.

The country's total production capacity is 3 million mt per annum, but output is far below this level. In 2009 domestic output was 1.9 million mt while consumption was 2.3 million mt, the gap being made up by net imports of more than 0.4 million mt (see Table 16.1 and Figure 16.1).

There are three cement manufacturers in Tanzania, all of which were formerly owned by the government and then privatized in the 1990s. All are now part of multinational cement groups (Table 16.2).

Lake Cement, a new entrant to the field, is setting up a plant in Lindi and plans to produce 500,000 mt per annum. Athi River Mining is constructing two plants, one in Tanga (Rhino Cement Ltd) with an installed capacity of 1,500,000 mt per annum and another in Coast Region (Mkuranga) with an annual capacity of 750,000 mt.

Paints.   There are several paint manufacturers in Tanzania, and between them they manufacture a wide range of paints for buildings, roads and vehicles.

Sadolin Paints (T) Ltd was established as part of Sadolin Paints (East Africa), which in turn was a subsidiary of Sadolin (Denmark). It has a well-developed countrywide network of distributors and its products include decorative, automotive and protective coating paints, varnishes, lacquers and enamels.

In 1985 Sadolin (Denmark) became part of the Akzo Nobel Paints & Coatings company, which decided to divest their interests in East Africa in 1991.

TABLE 16.1. Cement imports, exports, production and consumption.

Year	Imported	Exported	Production	Consumption
2000	7,281	30,497	833,092	809,876
2001	56,395	53,517	900,430	903,308
2002	149,079	37,203	1,026,082	1,137,958
2003	166,446	34,396	1,186,434	1,318,484
2004	125,007	37,655	1,280,851	1,368,203
2005	120,200	40,430	1,375,222	1,454,992
2006	92,711	98	1,421,460	1,514,073
2007	101,827	144	1,629,890	1,731,573
2008	356,468	99,688	1,755,862	2,012,642
2009P	516,182	57,569	1,940,845	2,399,458

Source: National Bureau of Statistics (2010): Statistical Abstract.

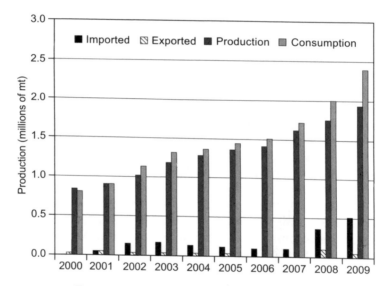

FIGURE 16.1. Cement production 2000–2009.
Source: National Bureau of Statistics (2010): Statistical Abstract.

Goldstar Paints Tanzania Limited is a long-established manufacturer that has produced decorative, automotive and industrial paints for more than two decades.

Insignia is allied with two international paint manufacturers: Marmoran (Pty) Ltd of South Africa and Pat's Deco of France. The company manufactures and markets a wide range of paints and allied products.

TABLE 16.2. Cement companies.

Company	Major shareholder	Location	Installed capacity (mt per annum)
Tanga Cement Company Limited	Holcim (Mauritius)	Tanga City	1,250,000
Tanzania Portland Cement Company Limited	Heidelberg Cement (Denmark)	Dar es Salaam	1,400,000
Mbeya Cement Company Limited	Lafarge (France)	Mbeya municipality	350,000
Total			3,000,000

TABLE 16.3. Major private industrial forest plantations.

	Planted area (hectares)	Land bank (hectares)
Mufindi Paper Mills	3,600	30–40,000
Tanganyika Wattle Co Ltd	14,500	Not available
Green Resources Ltd	8,500	30,000
Kilombero Valley Teak Company Ltd	8,148	28,232
The New Forest Company Ltd	1,400	4,000
Total	36,148	~100,000

Berger Paints International Limited was established in 1951 as Sherwood Paint Industries Ltd. It is the oldest paint company in the country. Berger Paints International is a global player with a strong presence in Asia, the Caribbean, the Pacific region, Africa and the Middle East.

Timber. Tanzania has over 33 million hectares of forest and woodland and 82,000 plantation forests. Sao Hill Plantation owns 50% of all plantation forests, and supplies 85% of the timber industry's raw material. There are five major private industrial forest plantations; their capacities are given in Table 16.3.

Tanzania produces a wide range of timber products, from both natural and plantation forests (see Table 16.4). During the socialist period, a number of parastatals dealt with the production of timber, parquet, utility poles, pulp and paper, joinery, construction and packaging, all under the name Tanzania Wood Industries Ltd. While some of these companies collapsed after nationalization, most still operate as medium-sized companies under private ownership. They include Sikh Saw Mills (T) Ltd and Tembo Chipboards Ltd of Tanga, Sao Hill Industries of Iringa and Kilimanjaro Timber

TABLE 16.4. Production of selected timber products: 2004–9.

Commodity	Unit	2004	2005	2006	2007	2008	2009P
Plywood	m^3	—	1,703	1,032	1,080	925	1,015
Timber	m^3	27,789	26,900	40,807	46,684	39,173	37,152
Chipboard	mt	2,042	1,942	2,400	2,400	2,140	2,106
Hard Board	mt	322	270	1,638	255	248	—

Source: National Bureau of Statistics (2010): Statistical Abstract.

Utilization Company of Moshi. There are also some new, predominantly small or medium-sized, private entrants. Total installed capacity is about 2.6 million cubic metres per annum, of which 83% is softwood and 17% is hardwood.

On the demand side, the main buyers (and the quantities that they consume annually in cubic metres) are Mufindi Paper Mills (250,000) and Sao Hills Industries (100,000). The rest (about 650,000 cubic metres in total) is used by hundreds of SMEs. Demand for timber has been increasing rapidly. A recent analysis estimates that there will be a large shortfall within the next 15 years.

Sand, aggregates and ready-mix concrete. Many small informal enterprises are involved in the supply of aggregates and sand to small contractors. Some medium-sized firms, including some building contractors, produce concrete blocks, aggregates, stones, murram, marble, terrazzo chips, base course materials, granite slabs and ready-mix concrete. Some also undertake concrete works, manufacture concrete culverts, paving blocks and hollow blocks.

Nyanza Road Works is part of Motisun Holdings (based in Mwanza) and is one of the country's largest producers of aggregates, bricks, concrete tiles and related building materials. It was founded on quarrying, which is still one of the company's activities. After years of involvement in drilling, blasting and the crushing of aggregates, the company decided to invest in a granite quarry on the outskirts of the city of Mwanza, at Nyang'homango. The aggregates produced are of various sizes required for road and building works. The company operates plants that produce concrete paving blocks, slabs and tiles of various types and colours. The strength and durability of these blocks and tiles is tested at the company's laboratories in order to ensure a quality product. The company also produces concrete roofing tiles, kerbstones, culverts for drainage and bricks. It has its own delivery vehicles, ensuring a rapid and efficient response to client requirements.

Other companies in the sector include Arusha Aggregates Ltd (based in Majengo Juu in Arusha) and Highland Estates Limited (based in Dar es Salaam.)

Precast products and tiles. Various types of tile for walls, flooring and roofing are manufactured by both medium-sized and small enterprises. The medium-sized firms include Mbezi Tiles Ltd (based in Dar es Salaam) and Tembo Tiles Ltd (located in Mikocheni). Some building contractors also manufacture and sell tiles.

Supply and marketing chain. Most raw materials for cement and building materials are obtained locally. Imported raw materials pass through Dar es Salaam and Tanga ports and are transported mainly by road, as the railway system is not currently functioning. Distribution is mainly through sales agents who sell to wholesalers and retailers.

Competitiveness. The cement and paint industries have adopted best-practice technologies, enabling them to compete effectively with imports. Tanga Cement Company Limited and Tanzania Cement Company have developed products that enable them to reduce production costs by using readily available low-cost materials without compromising quality. Tanzania is the lowest-cost cement producer in East Africa at US$160 per mt, and is ranked third in the whole of Africa after Egypt (US$92) and South Africa (US$134).

Policy context. In 2008 there was a brief cement shortage. This came about as a result of domestic cement factories exporting cement to South Africa for the construction of facilities for the 2010 FIFA World Cup. The government responded by zero rating cement, resulting in importation of 3.6 million mt of cement annually, some of which was re-exported. Since then, local producers have been lobbying for the suspended duty of 35% to be restored to restrict imports.

Challenges. The main challenges facing the cement and building materials sector are as follows.

- Energy constitutes 30–50% of the cost of cement. The cost of electricity in Tanzania has been rising, and the supply of power is erratic, forcing producers to rely on very expensive standby generators.
- Most of the factories use some imported raw materials, whose prices fluctuate widely with the exchange rate.
- There is strong competition from imports for some products (e.g. paints).

16.2   Profiles of Major Firms

16.2.1   Tanga Cement Company Ltd

Basic details. Tanga Cement Company has about 300 employees and annual sales of around US$100 million.

History. The process of establishing Tanga Cement Company began in 1975 and was spearheaded by the Tanzania Saruji Corporation, a public entity that had been created to promote the building materials sector in Tanzania. The factory was one of hundreds of industrial projects developed during the socialist era. At the time of its commissioning in 1980 the installed capacity was 500,000 mt per annum. The initial investment of US$115 million came from a combination of grants, the Treasury and a loan from the Tanzania Investment Bank.

Throughout the 1980s the company's performance was erratic. This was due to a shortage of foreign exchange to procure key inputs and to inadequate managerial capacity. Until 1989 the plant was managed by the Tanzania Saruji Corporation. In 1989 Holderbank of Switzerland, now Holcim Limited, was brought in to manage the plant under contract for five years in the run up to privatization. In 1996 Tanga Cement Company Limited was privatized, with a majority stake (60%) going to Holcim (Switzerland) and the rest remaining with the government. In 2002 the company was listed on the Dar es Salaam Stock Exchange. The current ownership is as follows: Afrisam Mauritius, 62.5%; the public, 35.4%; and employees, 2.1%.

In 2007 Tanga Cement Company commissioned a coal mill that enabled it to change from oil to coal firing. In 2010 it set up a second cement milling plant and a packing plant, thereby increasing its production and packing capacity to over 1,250,000 mt per annum. Sales have increased from US$40 million in 2000 to US$100 million in 2010.

Current activities and products. Tanga Cement Company produces two types of cement: a high-strength Portland composite with limestone additive and a normal-strength Portland composite with pozzolana and limestone additives.

Organization and management. The board of directors includes members from South Africa, Sweden and Tanzania. The company is organized into seven divisions: finance; plant management; sales and marketing; occupational health, safety and environment; human resources and administration; projects; and corporate communication.

Firm capabilities. The company has a formal quality assurance accreditation programme, with all operations following the ISO 9001:2008 system. It is also ISO 14001 certified, meeting international environmental standards. Tanga Cement Company has acquired a majority shareholding in Cement Distributors (EA) Ltd of Dar es Salaam, allowing it to become the only cement manufacturer in Tanzania that controls its entire supply chain: from mining of raw materials through manufacturing, packaging and transportation to the end user.

Supply and marketing chain. Limestone is sourced from the company's site at Pongwe, just outside Tanga city. Gypsum is mined from Makanya in the Kilimanjaro region and transported to the factory by trucks (the railway line to Tanga has been closed since 2009). (Since 2005, the company has been using pozzolana to supplement the need for clinker.) Coal is obtained from South Africa and from Songa in Tanzania. Tanga Cement Company has a long-term contract with Cement Distributors (EA) Ltd of Dar es Salaam, which operates 10 branches that sell to retailers and wholesalers. Cement is distributed to wholesale customers by truck. The use of road transport as opposed to rail to carry raw materials and cement has substantially increased operating costs.

Exports. The main export markets are Rwanda and Burundi, which take a combined total of about 40,000 mt per annum.

Development agenda. The firm's focus is now on achieving further improvements in productivity. Further expansion will depend on developments surrounding the high cost of transport due to the collapse of the railway system, and the provision of a reliable supply of electricity.

16.2.2   Tanzania Portland Cement Company Ltd (TPCCL)

Basic details. TPCCL, located 30 km from Dar es Salaam, currently employs 320 staff and had sales of US$130 million in 2010.

History. In 1962 Cementia Holdings AG of Switzerland, in collaboration with the Tanganyika Development Company (now the Tanzania Development Corporation), began construction of a cement factory at Wazo Hill in Dar es Salaam. The government of Tanzania held a 20% stake. Production began in 1966. In 1967 the government increased its share in TPCCL to 50%, and in 1973 the company was nationalized. In 1992 the government set up a joint venture with Scancem International ANS (which held 13% of TPCCL's shares) and Swedfund International AB (which also held 13%; the government held the remaining shares). TPCCL was privatized in 1998. As of 2005 the Tanzanian government held 30.0% of the company's shares and Scancem International held 69.3%. The firm's employees held the remaining 0.7%.

Due to the consolidation of Scancem International ANS into the HeidelbergCement Group of Germany, the former is now known as HeidelbergCement Africa (HC Africa). It owns, operates and manages cement factories, grinding plants and terminals, in addition to organizing the distribution and sale of its cement. The company operates in seven sub-Saharan countries; its head office is located in Oslo.

Current activities and products. The company manufactures aggregates and two brands of cement that conform to standards issued by the Tanzania Bureau of Standards: Twiga Ordinary and Twiga Extra. Bulk cement for large buyers is pumped into bulk tankers (trucks) with capacities of 20–30 mt. Both types of cement are supplied in 50 kg polypropylene bags. They are also supplied in 1.5 mt bags by prior arrangement.

Organization and management. The local management team in Tanzania has full responsibility for production, market development and human resources. They are supported by the group's Shared Service Centres, which bring together, at national level, the administrative functions for all the group's businesses based on standardized information technology infrastructure. HeidelbergCement standardizes management processes to ensure transparency and efficiency. Uniform group-wide key performance indicators allow benchmarking across businesses.

Firm capabilities. HeidelbergCement determines the firm's business model and ensures the use of state-of-the-art technology and management. It also sets a balance between local responsibility and group-wide standards. Since 2008 TPCCL has strengthened its level of service to the large contractors and other professional cement users that it supplies by expanding bulk handling capacity and increasing the number of its mobile silos. TPCCL is now also able to ensure increased and regular supplies up-country; sales in the Lake and Dodoma regions have grown substantially.

Supply and marketing chain. Distribution takes place through about a dozen wholesale agents, who in turn sell to sub-wholesalers and retailers.

Recent developments. TPCCL commissioned a US$100 million expansion project in 2009 that has made it independent of imported clinker. The expansion project involved a full production line with a screener/crusher for raw materials, limestone storage, a raw meal mill and silo, a five-stage cyclone pre-heater rotary kiln, a cement mill and silo, a packing and dispatch facility, and a dedicated 132 kV power line. It has now halted this expansion plan, however, because of a land dispute. It still intends to expand its current production capacity to 1.2 million mt per annum.

Chapter 17

METALS, ENGINEERING AND ASSEMBLY

17.1   Sector Profile

Background and overview. The 2009 Survey of Industrial Establishments by the National Bureau of Statistics identified 38 enterprises that deal with metals and fabricated metal products; ten of these enterprises were foreign owned and nine others were jointly owned with foreign firms. Only nine of the 38 had 100 or more employees. They employed around 3,200 people and had combined sales exceeding US$150 million, 5% of which came from exports.

Historical development. Aluminum Africa Ltd (now ALAF Ltd), Tanzania's leading steel and aluminium producer, was founded in 1960. It was nationalized in 1973 and privatized again in the 1990s.

Two of Tanzania's earliest steel companies, which produced re-enforcement bars (re-bar) for the construction industry, were established by the government under the auspices of the National Development Corporation. The National Steel Corporation, established in 1966, was sold in 2000 to New National Steel Ltd as a management and employee buyout. Steel Rolling Mills was founded in the early 1970s and was privatized in 2000: it was sold to a local company called Unique Group.

A wide range of steel products are produced in Tanzania: see Tables 17.1 and 17.2.

The steel, engineering and assembly sector comprises six groups of firms.

(1) Makers of steel and/or aluminium products from scrap.
(2) Steel and aluminium fabricators and body builders.
(3) Firms making drawn wire and related products.
(4) Vehicle body builders.
(5) Firms involved in the manufacture of large-scale steel and aluminium structures for the construction industry.
(6) Firms involved in steel or aluminium building projects.

TABLE 17.1. Major steel products and producers.

	Roofing sheets	Re-bar	Long products	Allied products
Aluminium Africa Ltd	✓			
MM Integrated Steel Mills	✓	✓	✓	✓
Sitta Steel Rolling Ltd		✓	✓	
Kamal Steel	✓			
Tanzania Steel Pipes Ltd			✓	
Sayona Steel Rolling Mills	✓			
Nyakato Steel Mills Ltd			✓	

Source: Interviews with sector actors.

TABLE 17.2. Steel and assembly production: 2006–10.

Products	2006	2007	2008	2009
Rolled steel (thousands of mt)	44	36	40	35
Iron sheets (thousands of mt)	30	36	32	51
Aluminum (mt)	105	110	105	58
Wire products (thousands of mt)	11	9	9	8
Galvanized pipes (thousands of mt)	6	7	8	9
Motor bodies and trailers (pieces)	136	184	214	183

Source: National Bureau of Statistics (2011).

Group 1: makers of steel and/or aluminium products from scrap.

Aluminum Africa Ltd (now ALAF Ltd) is based in Dar es Salaam and is the nucleus of the aluminium and steel sector in the country. It is profiled in the next section.

Sayona Steel Limited was incorporated in 2006 to manufacture metal products from scrap metal and billets. It is profiled in the next section.

Kamal Steel Ltd manufactures steel from scrap. It is profiled in the next section.

MM Integrated Steel Mills Ltd was established in 1995 and has an installed capacity of 24,000 mt of reinforcement bars, black pipes, galvanized pipes, hollow rectangular pipes, square pipes, flat bars, angles, cold-rolled coils and zinc galvanized coils per annum. It has a market share of 35% in roofing sheets.

Sita Steel Rollings Ltd, established in 1996, manufactures hollow sections, black pipes, z-purlins and cut-to-measure mild steel plates. The manufacturing plant of Sita Steel Rollings produces pipes up to 25 cm in diameter. The company is also an importer of related steel products.

Steel Masters Ltd has a furnace with a capacity of 60 mt per day and a rolling mill with a capacity of 60 mt per day. It produces ingots from scrap, which are either used in the rolling mill or sold to other local rolling mills. It also imports mild steel billets for use in its rolling mill for producing large angles, flat bars, HT bars, MSD form bars and round bars.

Nyakato Steel Mills Ltd, established in 1999, specializes in the manufacture of long products. Its main markets are in the Lake Zone region, and it exports to Kenya, Uganda, the Democratic Republic of the Congo, Rwanda and Burundi.

Trishalla Steel Rolling Mills is an iron and steel recycling factory based in the Arusha region. It is part of Sita Steel Rollings Ltd. It collects over 1,000 mt of scrap metal per month and employed more than 400 workers in 2010. It imports billets and scrap metal, from which it produces angled iron, mild steel plates and black pipes, round bars, deformed bars, square bars, flat bars and zed bars. Over 20% of its output is exported to Kenya.

Group 2: steel and aluminium fabricators and body builders.

Veercom Technical Ltd is a fabricator of mild steel plates. The company is engaged in cutting, bending and rolling, the making of chimneys, and the ducting of boilers.

National Engineering Company Limited is a leading engineering firm dealing with the design, manufacture and installation of steel structures and with mechanical and machine engineering. It was founded in 1967 jointly by Twentsche Overseas Trading Co. and Sarantis & Panayatopoulus Company Limited and it was subsequently nationalized. In 1997 Mideast Trading Agencies of Jeddah, Saudi Arabia, acquired National Engineering Company from the government of Tanzania.

Group 3: makers of drawn wire and related products.

ChemiCotex Industries Ltd, established in 1975, is based in Dar es Salaam. It manufactures a wide range of products, including barbed wire, chain link fencing, expanded metal and nails. It is part of the Mac Group.

Group 4: vehicle body builders.

Yusufali and Sons Ltd is the leading body builder in Tanzania, specializing in the manufacture of truck bodies.

Nanak Body Builders Ltd specializes in the fabrication of truck bodies, water tanks, fuel tanks and underground tanks. Established by Mr Gian Singh Jheetey in 1980, it employs between 15 and 50 people at a time and has annual sales of around US$1 million.

Group 5: makers of large-scale structures.

Bitec International Company Limited is a mechanical construction company. It has some 15–20 full-time employees and as many as 50 casual employees at a time. It had a turnover of US$500,000 in 2010.

The firm was established in 2005 by Michael Shimiyu, an engineer who had previously worked in senior management positions with a number of engineering firms. In 1996, while working with Caltex Oil (T) Ltd, he was invited by Ingra Engineering to assist in the development of its newly franchised construction operations in Tanzania. It was on the basis of his experience in this venture that he went on to establish Bitec International Company.

Bitec International Company undertakes the design, fabrication and erection of steel structures. These include petroleum and oil depots and terminals, refueling service stations, steel roof structures and buildings. Refurbishment works include tank cleaning and repairs, demolition and decontamination of toxic materials, pipelines and structural repairs, sandblasting and repainting. The company also performs civil works related to the erection of steel structures.

Group 6: makers of steel and aluminium products for the construction industry.

Shamo Group has grown from a small enterprise in Somalia in the early 1970s to a multinational group of companies active in the UAE, Tanzania and Zambia. It was founded by Mr Abucar Amin, whose first business enterprise was a hardware store specializing in the importation and sale of building materials. The company began operations in Tanzania in 1992.

The firm's main products in Tanzania are aluminium and glass systems, steel/aluminium doors, windows, partitions, shop fronts, curtain walls, flush glazing, concrete roofing tiles, concrete cement pavers and PVC pipes. The firm also supplies fixed suspended ceilings.

Tanzania Steel Pipes Limited is a Chinese-owned company established in 2004. It acquired the then government owned Ubungo Farm Implements in the same year, under the privatization scheme, and transformed it into a manufacturer of large-diameter plastic and steel water pipes and fittings. It imports some products from China, including machinery for

TABLE 17.3. Steel imports (thousands of mt).

Imports	2001	2002	2003	2004	2005	2006	2007	2008	2009
Ingots and semis	19	13	24	12	12	1	1	3	10
Long products	33	29	27	34	47	65	57	101	143
Flat products	66	87	90	120	138	136	136	135	43
Tubular products	2	4	22	2	5	6	6	13	8

Source: International Steel Institute (2010).

manufacturing steel pipes for sale in the domestic and re-export market. It exports to Rwanda, Burundi, the Democratic Republic of the Congo, Zambia and Uganda.

Imports. Steel production does not meet market demand, and the quality of steel produced in Tanzania does not meet ISO standards. Imports have been increasing (see Table 17.3). The main sources of imported steel are Turkey, South Africa, Japan, Russia and Belgium.

Policy context. Imported steel carries an import duty of 25%: a measure designed to protect the local industry. Export of scrap metal is prohibited, but steel manufacturers report that scrap metal is exported illegally in large quantities. The government has decided to encourage the exploitation of iron ore deposits in Mchuchuma.

Challenges. The main challenges facing the sector are as follows.

- A shortage of scrap metal, which is forcing manufacturers to import scrap from South Africa and South Korea.
- The quality of locally produced steel is poor. Some industry stakeholders are concerned that the National Bureau of Standards might not be playing an effective role in this regard. However, steel producers maintain that their products meet the requisite industry standards.
- Expensive and unreliable power supply.
- Poor transport infrastructure (roads and the dysfunctional railway system), occasioning high transport costs and delays.
- Inadequate and inefficient port services.
- Stakeholders in the sector complain of widespread corruption.

Recent developments. The government of Tanzania recently signed a US$3 billion coal and steel mining agreement with the Chinese mining conglomerate Sichuan Hongda Group that will offer a major opportunity in the generation of coal-fired electricity. This agreement could also lead to the development of a sizeable iron and steel industry in Tanzania.

Studies by the National Development Corporation indicate that the Liganga area is rich in minerals containing iron, vanadium and titanium. Reserves are estimated to be between 200 and 1,200 million mt, with reserves of 45 million mt already proven through drilling. Pilot projects have shown that the iron ore can be smelted by the Elkem or Krupp–Renn processes to produce acceptable low-titanium iron.

17.2 Profiles of Major Firms

17.2.1 ALAF Ltd

Basic details. Aluminum Africa Ltd (now ALAF Ltd) was established in 1960 by the Chandaria Group. It is currently jointly owned by SAFAL Investments (Mauritius) Limited (76%) and the government of Tanzania (24%). ALAF employs about 550 workers and has an annual turnover of about US$100 million.

History. The main shareholder in the SAFAL Group is Dr Manu Chandaria. The Chandaria Group was established in the mid 1950s by Dr Chandaria's father (who moved from India to Kenya in 1916) as a merchant running a provisions store. He entered manufacturing by buying into an aluminium plant, KaluWorks. Manu Chandaria worked initially in his father's provisions store in Nairobi, before studying engineering in the US. Subsequently he joined the family business. The group has, over time, acquired plants across several continents.

ALAF was set up by the Chandaria Group in 1960 and was the first company in Tanzania to operate a sheet-to-sheet galvanizing line. The company was nationalized in 1973, with the government taking 62.5% of the shares. Comcraft Services Limited was appointed to manage the firm and this arrangement continued until 1988, when the management contract was terminated and ALAF was placed under the auspices of the National Development Corporation.

As part of the process of divestiture of parastatals, the Comcraft Group became the majority shareholder in ALAF.

In 1997 ALAF returned to the Chandaria Group when Chandaria's subsidiary, SAFAL Investment (Mauritius), acquired 76% of the shares. The SAFAL Group is the leading manufacturer of flat and long steel products in Africa. It was established in 1995 and produces cold-rolled, galvanized,

TABLE 17.4. ALAF: selected product lines.

	Division	Main products
Coils	STEELCO	• Cold-rolled steel coils and sheets
	Metal Coating Line	• Aluminium and zinc coated steel coils
Roofing	PIPECO	• Steel pipes • Square and rectangular hollow sections
	ALUCO	• Aluminum plain, corrugated and profiled roofing sheets • Aluminium for kitchenware

aluminium–zinc coated and pre-painted steel coils that conform to international standards in its world-class manufacturing facilities across East and Southern Africa.

Current activities and products. ALAF operates through two main product divisions: one manufactures coils and the other processes these coils into final products (Table 17.4).

ALAF also imports and distributes a wide range of steel products.

Organization and management. ALAF's chief operating officer is assisted by two general managers (coils and roofing) and by functional heads for human resources, finance, information technology and logistics.

Firm capabilities. ALAF's technology enables it to produce products that are suitable as long-lasting roofing in the Tanzanian environment. Some products are based on a proprietary technology that combines the corrosion-resistant properties of zinc and aluminium, making the roofing sheets maintenance free. A wide range of colours is available.

ALAF has undertaken many large roofing projects, including the Mlimani City Shopping Centre and Conference Centre at Dar es Salaam, the Arusha International Conference Centre in Arusha, and the Prime Minister's Complex in Dodoma.

Supply and marketing chain. Hot rolled steel coils, aluminium–silicon alloy and zinc are imported from Japan, Russia, Europe and India. ALAF has a countrywide distribution network of wholesalers who sell to retail hardware stores. The company's main bases are located in Dar es Salaam, Arusha and Mwanza. The firm exports by road to Zambia, Rwanda, Burundi, Malawi, Mozambique, Angola and the Democratic Republic of the Congo.

Recent developments. In 2009 ALAF commissioned a new state-of-the-art metal coating line for producing aluminium and zinc coated steel coils, which are then profiled as roofing sheets. The technology for this line was provided by a US-based equipment supplier. In 2011 it set up a new state-of-the-art pipe mill for producing pipes, and cut and bend machines for producing re-bar.

17.2.2 Kamal Steel Ltd

Basic details. Kamal Steel manufactures steel from scrap. It employs 600 people and has an annual turnover of US$9–10 million.

History. Gagan Gupta, the chairman of Kamal Steel, came to Tanzania from India in 2004 and established Kamal Steel to manufacture steel from scrap. Mr Gupta's family had been involved in trading activities in India for generations. On graduating as an engineer he entered the family's Indian business, and in 1993 he began operating as a steel stockholder in the Agra area under the name Kamal Enterprises. In 1997 he decided to enter manufacturing in India, setting up a steel furnace to produce steel from recycled scrap. In the 1990s Kamal Enterprises became the first firm in India to manufacture steel from sponge iron. By the time Mr Gupta began his Tanzanian venture, Kamal Enterprises was well established as a steel producer in India.

Mr Gupta's move to Tanzania was initiated during a visit to London by a fortuitous remark by a business associate, who put it to him that there was great scope for building a steel business in Tanzania. This prompted Mr Gupta to take a family vacation in Tanzania, and he subsequently decided to set up a business there. He still retains a share in his original Indian business, and spends a moderate fraction of his time in India.

His Tanzanian business grew quickly and in 2007 he added a second mill. A year later he set up his own air separation plant, which allowed him to produce oxygen for his mill on site. The firm is currently in the process of building a new greenfield operation that will raise its capacity twenty-fold: from its present 35–40,000 mt per annum to 700,000 mt per annum, at an investment cost of US$200 million. The mill is being installed on a turnkey basis, using Italian equipment, by Electro-Therm of India.

Current activities and products. Some 80% of the firm's current output consist of re-bar for the construction industry, while the remaining 20% comprises flat bar and angles. The new plant will be devoted wholly to the production of re-bar.

Organization and management.   The firm is wholly owned and managed by Mr Gupta.

Supply and marketing chain.   The main raw material is locally sourced steel scrap. The export of scrap from Tanzania is illegal but illicit trade is substantial and poses a serious potential threat to the viability of the new enterprise. It is possible that the firm will be forced to import scrap steel at world prices to achieve its planned level of operation.

All sales of re-bar are, at present, to the domestic construction industry, but the new plant will permit the firm to export substantial volumes to neighbouring countries.

Recent developments.   The firm is now in the process of establishing three new businesses: a refinery to recycle waste oil, an agribusiness in pulses, and a plant for the manufacture of electrical transmission and distribution panels.

In establishing a site, near Dar es Salaam, for its new operation, the company has purchased land far in excess of the plant's own needs, allowing it to set up a large (113 hectare) industrial estate on which local businesses can take out leases on fully serviced plots, ready for immediate occupancy.

17.2.3   Sayona Steel Limited

Basic details.   Sayona Steel, located in the Mwanza region, is one of the leading steel mills in Tanzania. The company is part of the Demeter Group, which has various interests in Tanzania, Kenya, Zambia, Mozambique and Zimbabwe. The installed capacity of Sayona Steel is over 2,400 mt per annum and it has more than 100 employees.

History.   The history of the Demeter Group dates back to 1973, when Mr Prem Kapoor established Auto Spares Mwanza Limited, a retail seller of automotive spare parts. Other trading businesses were established later in fertilizers, pesticides, agricultural inputs, human and veterinary health, cotton ginning, coffee processing, organic vanilla farming and processing, hot steel rolling and manufacturing, sisal farming and processing, commodity trading and processing and cultivation of Artemisia for anti-malarial medicine. Sayona Steel Limited is a recent addition, having been incorporated in 2006.

Current activities and products.   Sayona Steel manufactures re-bar from scrap metal and billets. It also produces made-to-measure mild steel plates and galvanized sheet.

The other activities of the group are as follows.

Lintex (Tanzania) Ltd, established in 1995, is a ginnery that buys and processes seed cotton. The ginnery comprises 26 jumbo roller gins with a capacity to produce 250 bales per day during the season (each bale weighs 220 kg). Towards the end of the cotton season, the company buys yellow grams, green grams, and so on from the farmer (who normally uses the land to grow these crops after the cotton crop is finished). The purchased grams are usually exported to India and the Middle East.

Mara Coffee Ltd processes and exports approximately 2,000 mt per annum of conventional hard arabica coffee, mostly to European markets.

The group also has subsidiaries in cashew nut and vanilla cultivation and in real estate.

Organization and management. The chief executive of Sayona Steel reports to the board of directors of the Demeter Group. The group sets targets and budgets, performs audits and oversees the heads of each company in the group.

Firm capabilities. Sayona Steel, having begun as a maker of re-bar, expanded its activities by adding a galvanizing and cold-rolling plant in 2009.

Exports. Sayona Steel exported US$1 million of goods in 2010, mostly re-bar to the Democratic Republic of the Congo.

Chapter 18

PLASTIC, GLASS AND PAPER

18.1   Sector Profile I: Plastics

A 2009 survey of manufacturing firms by the National Bureau of Statistics identified 41 producers of rubber, plastics and non-mineral products in Tanzania, nine of which were foreign owned and five of which were owned jointly with a foreign partner. Of the 41 firms only 12 employed more than 100 people (classifying them as large firms). About a third (16) of the identified companies commenced operations after 2000. Total combined exports in 2008 amounted to US$523 million. The sector employs around 6,800 people in total.

Because of competition from imports, the sector has been working below capacity. Capacity utilization was 48% in 2008.

Profiles and lines of business of large firms.

Sumaria Holdings owns four companies in the plastics industry.

(i) Tanzania Plastic Industries was established in 1975. It produces household plastic goods, furniture and rubber footwear.

(ii) Simba Plastics Tanzania was acquired by Sumaria Holdings in 1975. This acquisition was followed by subsequent brownfield expansions into injection, blow moulding and film extrusion.

(iii) Sumaria Industries Limited, established in 1979, employs more than 300 people. Sumaria Industries produces a broad range of products, from rigid packaging for multinational firms to products for the retail consumer market. It has invested in injection moulding, tubing, extruders and injection blow equipment, and complex stack moulds; it also has an in-house mould-making facility.

(iv) DPI Simba Ltd manufactures PVC and polyethylene pipes for the civil engineering, mining, construction and agricultural sectors. It is the largest manufacturer and marketer of PVC water reticulation, drainage piping systems and fittings in East and Central Africa.

Jambo Plastics Ltd is a fast-growing company that deals with plastic injection and blow moulding products. It began operating in 1996 with just a few machines, but it now has more than 50 machines incorporating the latest technology; it has a processing capacity approaching 1,500 mt per month. The company is led by engineers and professionals from the Central Institute of Plastic Engineering and Technology in India. It is a leading manufacturer and exporter of plastic household ware, moulded furniture and industrial containers.

Centaza Industries Ltd specializes in the manufacture of packaging materials in various materials (HDPE, low-density polyethylene and polypropylene) for industrial packaging. Its products include unplasticized polyvinyl chloride pipes, HDPE coils, gutter profiles and fittings, bags for consumer goods, exploratory mining and garbage disposal. It also has facilities to co-extrude multilayer low-density polyethylene.

Cello Industries Ltd manufactures plastic household goods and furniture. It is profiled in Section 18.4.1 below.

Profiles and lines of business of medium-sized firms.

The Motisun Holdings group owns three companies in the industry.

MM Industries Limited–Kiboko PVC manufactures water storage tanks, unplasticized polyvinyl chloride pipes, HDPE pipes and coils, PET bottles, buckets and shrink film. The company employs 47 people.

MM Industries Limited–Kiboko Water Tank manufactures water tanks. It employs 39 people.

MM Industries Limited–PET Plant produces plastic bottles and containers. It employs 68 people.

East Star International Tanzania Ltd, a family business established in 2007, makes plastic shoes. The business employs between 100 and 150 people and has annual sales of about US$1 million.

Other manufactures include African Polymers Tanzania, C & C Industries Ltd, ChemiCotex Industries Ltd, East Africa Pipes Limited, Falcon Industries Limited, Metro Plastic Industries Limited, Suchack Plastics Limited, Multi Cable Limited, Nabaki Africa Limited, Plasco Limited, Printo Wrappings Limited, Reni International and Unoplast (T) Limited.

Challenges.   The main challenges facing the plastic sector are as follows.

- The excise duty in Tanzania is 120% whereas in Kenya it is 50%, making Tanzanian products more costly and hence less competitive in the regional market.

- Stringent standards are applied to locally made products but not to imports. The Tanzania Bureau of Standards has produced 39 standards for plastics alone.
- Costly and unreliable power supply.
- Slow and costly port clearance processes. All raw materials for plastics are imported. The process of clearing raw materials from the port normally takes 21 days (and can even take 30 days).

18.2   Sector Profile II: Glass

Kioo Limited, a subsidiary of the Madhvani Group of Uganda, established the first glass factory in Tanzania in 1965. In the 1980s the government set up a second glass factory—the Mbagala Sheet Glass Company Limited—but this was never commissioned. Several large and medium-sized firms are now active in Tanzania in the production of glass, mostly producing containers and building materials. Glass production has been increasing steadily since 2005, partly as a result of growth in the construction sector and a shift in favour of glass for interior walls and partitions.

Kioo Limited employs 247 people and had a turnover of more than US$21 million in 2010. The company has forward and backward linkages with the economy: over 80% of its raw materials (sand, dolomite and feldspar) are sourced locally and it supplies beverage and liquor firms and some pharmaceutical companies with packing materials. Kioo exports about 60% of its products to sub-Saharan countries. Prior to 2005 its glass sales had declined substantially. This trend was reversed after Tanzania Breweries Limited supported Kioo in upgrading its technology and entered into a long-term supply contract with the firm.

Dar es Salaam Glassworks (DGW) employs more than 200 workers. It is profiled in Section 18.4.4 below.

Profiles and lines of business of medium-sized firms.

Aluminum City Limited operates an aluminium and glass works that supplies structural products: aluminium doors, windows, partitions made from aluminium profiles, sheet glass, laminated glass, sand blast glass, glass furniture and decorative glass. It is owned by Quality Group Limited.

Selebhai Glass and Aluminum Ltd manufactures laminated safety glass and fabricated aluminium doors and windows. It employs about 50 people.

18.3   Sector Profile III: Paper

In 1986 the government established a large forest plantation and set up Mufindi Paper Mills Ltd in the Iringa region. This is still the only paper producer in the country. It was envisaged at that time that most of the mill's output would be exported. However, capacity utilization remained very low until the company was privatized in the 1990s. Mufindi Paper Mills is an integrated plantation-pine-based pulp and paper mill with a capacity of 140,000 mt per annum. It is profiled in Section 18.4.3 below.

Challenges facing the paper sector include the following.

- Costly and unreliable power supply. This has forced Mufindi Paper Mills to establish its own source of power: by recycling its paper byproducts.
- Competition from imports. The industry has been facing serious competition from cheaper imports. Mufindi Paper Mills is reported to be lobbying the government to increase the import duty on paper.
- High transport costs, especially from the production area to the ports and consumption areas, due to unreliable and inadequate railway services.

18.4   Profiles of Major Firms

18.4.1   Cello Industries Tanzania Ltd

Basic details. Cello Industries Tanzania manufactures a wide range of plastics products. It employs 400 workers and has a turnover of about US$2 million.

History. The firm was founded by three partners in 2004. It began with five machines and 50 employees. Prior to founding Cello Industries Tanzania the partners had operated a trading company importing pens, rulers and laundry baskets from India. They realized that while domestic demand for plastics products was growing, the imported products available on the market were of low quality and were relatively expensive. Local production was in the hands of a small number of firms. A market study revealed a substantial potential for local manufacturing. Cello Industries Tanzania was founded by the three partners with technical assistance from Cello India: one of the suppliers to their import business. The company's first products were chairs and tableware, which were sold at around a dollar less than the imported competition. The firm carried out a major expansion in 2007/08.

Current activities and products. Cello Industries Tanzania manufactures a wide variety of tableware, chairs, kitchen and household plastics. In total they produce 800 different products.

Organization and management. The three original founders own and manage the firm.

Firm capabilities. Cello Industries Tanzania operates 40 plastic-moulding machines, using 800 different moulds. Colours and designs can be slightly modified to suit individual buyers.

Supply and marketing chain. Raw materials are imported mainly from India. Most of the finished products are collected by buyers at the factory. Cello Industries Tanzania also distributes its products within the domestic market, via its fleet of 40 vans.

Most of what is exported is bought in Dar es Salaam by foreign distributors. Goods are shipped by sea to Zimbabwe, Kenya, Mozambique, Dubai, the Democratic Republic of the Congo, Rwanda and Burundi. Cello Industries Tanzania provides export/import logistics services for those importers that are not familiar with the intricacies of passing through the port of Dar es Salaam.

Exports. Cello Industries Tanzania began its export business when the partners discovered that some of their customers were exporting their products to neighbouring countries. Almost 30% of the company's products are exported, either directly or indirectly. The main export destinations are Zimbabwe, Mozambique, Dubai, Kenya, Rwanda, Burundi and the Democratic Republic of the Congo. Exports to the EAC are duty free; exports to other markets face tariffs of 10%. In 2009, the firm accounted for 9% of Tanzania's (official) plastic exports.

Challenges. Lead times for delivery of spare parts are very long, and there is a lack of qualified technicians to carry out repairs.

18.4.2 *East Star International Tanzania Ltd*

Basic details. East Star International Tanzania is a family business, owned by Mr Jack Bu and his wife Li Wang, that manufactures plastic shoes. The business employs between 100 and 150 people and has annual sales of about US$1 million.

History.   Mr Jack Bu was born in China and he grew up and studied there. He set up a trading business in China and became involved in exporting plastic shoes to Tanzania. As a result he became familiar with the market for shoes in Tanzania. Noticing that imported shoes from China were of low quality, he decided to establish a shoe factory in Tanzania, commencing production in 2007. The initial investment was financed by a Chinese government scheme that supports new projects by Chinese investors in Africa.

Current activities and products.   The company produces plastic shoes (mainly sandals). Two sister companies are in operation: Lara Industries Ltd employs 30–50 people in the production of kitchen utensils (plates, cups, trays) using animal bones; Novo Industries Ltd, which also makes plastic shoes, employs about 20 people.

Organization and management.   The two owners act as managing director and deputy managing director. They employ a mix of Chinese and Tanzanian managers.

Firm capabilities.   The main strength of the company lies in its modern, automated machinery. The company has in place a good network of wholesalers and retailers from its earlier engagement in trading.

Supply and marketing chain.   Plastic powder is procured directly from large plastics manufacturers in China, as are moulds. The company has developed relations with an extensive network of wholesalers in Kigoma, Mara, Mbeya and Kariakoo (Dar es Salaam).

Challenges.   A key challenge facing manufacturing firms in Tanzania is erratic supply of electricity. The company uses a standby generator.

Development agenda.   The business is now planning to diversify into new plastics products. It hopes to grow to employ 300–500 people over the next five years.

18.4.3   *Mufindi Paper Mills (MPM) Limited*

Basic details.   MPM is an integrated, plantation-pine-based pulp and paper mill. Located in the Iringa region, it is by far the country's largest paper manufacturing company, with an annual capacity of 140,000 mt. The company employs more than 500 people. Its annual turnover fluctuates widely from year to year but is between US$25 million and US$100 million.

History. MPM began as a government-owned company called Southern Paper Mills. Commissioned in 1986, it initially operated at no more than about half of its installed capacity. Over the years output fell further: from around 10,000 mt per annum between 1991 and 1995, to just over 5,000 mt in 1996, and then to 1,800 mt in 1997. In 2004 Rai Group Limited of Kenya acquired the mill for US$1 million and embarked on a modernization process, investing US$40 million. A second phase of investment was completed using an US$80 million long-term loan from the Development Bank of Southern Africa.

Current activities and products. MPM's main products are packaging materials of various grades and specifications, including Kraft Liner, Sack Kraft, Bag Kraft, Deckle and Grammage.

Organization and management. The board of directors comprises a group of experienced professionals from Kenya, India and Tanzania. The managing director is assisted by a deputy general manager and departmental managers for production, marketing and sales, finance and administration, human resources, warehouse and shipping.

Firm capabilities. MPM has established plantations on 5,000 of the 20,000 hectares of land that it owns. It is also in the process of looking for additional land.

The company has invested in a 35.6 MW biomass power plant project, which enables it to meet its energy needs without being affected by the recurrent power shedding and without needing to use expensive power generators.

Supply and marketing chain. Wood comes from the factory's plantation in Mgololo. Major customers (from the paper, printing and packaging industries) collect their products in bulk from the factory. Distribution to other users is through a network of local wholesalers and export merchants.

Exports. The firm exports paper to Kenya, Uganda, Malawi, Zambia, India, Sri Lanka, Bangladesh, Malaysia, Vietnam, Iran, Egypt and Saudi Arabia.

Development agenda. MPM expects to invest more than US$170 million in its facilities over the next seven years (with funds raised from outside investors) in order to raise production capacity to meet growing demand in East African markets. The aim is to increase capacity to 150,000 mt per annum. The first phase of a planned expansion project is scheduled for completion by March 2013, with a second phase scheduled to finish by March 2017.

18.4.4   Dar es Salaam Glassworks Ltd

Basic details.   DGW employs more than 200 workers.

History.   DGW was founded by Mr Shiraz Jessa, who had previously owned a small firm selling louver glasses. He moved into manufacturing by setting up DGW, which was incorporated in 1979.

Current activities and products.   DGW is one of the leading firms in the manufacture, supply and installation of aluminium and glass. It specializes in building glass, architectural aluminium, door and window systems, curtain walling and structural glazing, wall cladding partitions, ceilings, metal roofing, skylight domes and associated products. Based in Dar es Salaam, the company undertakes projects from design through to manufacture and installation. It produces laminated glass for roofs and partition walls in shopping arcades, theatres and public buildings. DGW provides structural glazing with European reflective glass. The company's other products include cladding, Spider system, aluminium doors, windows, partitions, toughened glass, ceilings, sun breakers, balustrade and vertical blinds.

Organization and management.   The founder, who acts as managing director, takes responsibility for planning, contract negotiation and new business generation. Professional managers run the technical, marketing, finance and administrative areas.

Firm capabilities.   DGW's plant has aluminium, steel fabrication and glass processing machinery. DGW has links with Hunter Douglass, an international industrial group engaged in the manufacture and marketing of interior and exterior architectural products. DGW also has a technical tie-up with Aluminum Group (AG) of Italy, one of Europe's leading architectural and structural aluminium technology firms. The company also works with Prime Structures Engineering, a design and build engineering company based in Singapore.

Supply and marketing chain.   DGW has extensive relationships with domestic and foreign suppliers (in India and Europe) of both raw materials and technical expertise.

Development agenda.   DGW is currently installing a new plant line for the lamination and toughening of glass, with a modern furnace, which will produce glass with thermal insulation.

IGC International Growth Centre

The International Growth Centre aims to promote sustainable growth in developing countries by providing demand-led policy advice based on frontier research. Based at London School of Economics (LSE) and in partnership with Oxford University, the IGC is initiated and funded by the UK Department for International Development.

The IGC has active country programmes in Bangladesh, Ethiopia, Ghana, India (Central and Bihar), Mozambique, Pakistan, Rwanda, Sierra Leone, South Sudan, Tanzania, Uganda and Zambia and supports over 200 individual research projects on issues of governance, human capital, agriculture, infrastructure, trade, firm capabilities, state capacity, macroeconomics, finance and climate change.

The IGC is directed by a Steering Group that consists of two Academic Directors – one from the London School of Economics and one from Oxford University – as well as leading academics from prestigious British and American universities.

Contact us:

International Growth Centre
London School of Economics and Political Science
4th Floor
Tower Two
Houghton Street
London WC2A 2AE
United Kingdom

www.theigc.org

+44 (0)20 7955 6144

For all enquiries, please contact
Mazida Khatun: mazida.khatun@theigc.org